GHOSTS OF WESSEX

REGIONAL GHOST SERIES

GHOSTS
OF WESSEX

Keith B. Poole

DAVID & CHARLES
Newton Abbot   London
North Pomfret (VT)   Vancouver

for Keith Steadman

ISBN 0 7153 7287 4

Set in 11 on 13pt Linotype Baskerville and printed in
Great Britain by Latimer Trend & Company Ltd Plymouth
for David & Charles (Publishers) Limited
Brunel House   Newton Abbot   Devon

Published in the United States of America
by David & Charles Inc
North Pomfret   Vermont 05053   USA

Published in Canada
by Douglas David & Charles Limited
1875 Welch Street   North Vancouver   BC

CONTENTS

CONTENTS

ACKNOWLEDGEMENTS

I wish to express my gratitude to all the many libraries who have given me courtesy and service, especially those of Chelmsford and Reading; in particular to Miss Pool of the Reading Reference Library, whose help and advice in the initial research was invaluable. I am deeply grateful to my late brother Geoffrey, who though not in harmony with any form of the occult, did all he could to help in the research. My thanks also to Mrs Dorothy Miller; to Mr Gus Edwards; and to Mr Clifford Morris, the genial custodian at Rycote Chapel, for his assistance and permission to quote from his booklets.

It would be impossible to thank Madeline Paul adequately for her constant, untiring help and encouragement; for typing, checking, proof reading and endless verification. Without such help the book could never have emerged from its ghostly world into the reality of print.

BISHAM ABBEY

The Negative Ghost

Haunted, thirteenth-century Bisham Abbey stands on the Berkshire side of the Thames, upstream from Marlow. It is backed by the magnificent line of Quarry Woods, and has one of the most attractive settings in England. Its walls of chalk, flint, stone and brick give it a mellow colour which contrasts harmoniously with the dominant green of the great trees and lawns which run almost to the water's edge. It is occupied today by the Central Council of Physical Recreation.

The number of supernatural appearances in and around the abbey is quite considerable and frequent. Only recently two boys who had spent an evening quietly fishing along the river were returning along the towpath towards Bisham when they saw a boat between the abbey and the church. This was not, of course, unusual, but in the boat sat the figure of a very old lady dressed all in black. Like everyone else locally, the two boys knew the ancient Hoby legend and fled in sheer terror. More recently, the same figure has been seen between Bisham and the adjoining hamlet of Temple, not in a boat but walking. Had the boys seen the figure of a man instead of a woman in the boat, there might have been an explanation. Legend has it that an amorous squire eloped with the daughter of the Earl of Salisbury while he was at prayer, but was caught in a boat between Marlow and Bisham and locked up in a tower from which he escaped by leaping to the ground below and killing himself.

Some of the original abbey buildings still stand, notably the superb, fourteenth-century, vaulted entrance porch.

There is also the impressive, lofty Great Hall used by the Knights Templar when they first founded their preceptory here in the reign of King Stephen, and where they remained until their suppression by Edward II. 'Their good name being slandered', he put the abbey into private hands.

In this great hall with its armorial windows and splendid fireplace hangs the large portrait of Lady Hoby, the cause of all the trouble and the hauntings of the abbey since her death in 1609. It shows all too clearly her aristocratic, arrogant, chalk-white face and hands, plainly revealing her as a woman accustomed to command, to be obeyed, and intolerant of any form of stupidity. She is dressed in the contemporary coif, wimple, and weeds of a knight's widow, whereas her ghost appears always as a photographic negative would show it, her hands and face black, her costume white. So many witnesses have seen it throughout the centuries since her death, vouching for this transposition, that it is quite impossible to doubt them, nor the fear she always brings when she appears.

Before she came to live in the abbey, however, much history had passed there. Henry VIII, when dissolving the monasteries, threw the Augustinian monks out, then re-founded it as a Benedictine order, on condition the abbot and brethren prayed constantly for the soul of Jane Seymour, Henry's third wife, whom it is said he truly loved. Perhaps because he did not consider the prayers effective enough, Henry suppressed the abbey again within two years. He had by then got rid of 'the Flemish mare', as he so ungraciously called his ugly Dutch wife, Anne of Cleves, giving her a pension of £3,000 a year and throwing in Bisham Abbey for good measure. As Anne's alternative might have been the block, she accepted her fate but Henry died before attaching his seal of confirmation to the document, leaving her in a very uncertain position.

When Edward VI became king he ordered Anne to exchange the abbey for a house in Kent belonging to Sir Philip Hoby. The king, being in need of good counsellors, considered Berkshire to be nearer than Kent for his purposes. Anne was furious but had to yield, and in 1552 Sir Philip moved in to Bisham. He at once began to build a magnificent house, compatible with his high rank as English ambassador to most of the foreign courts and his very considerable wealth. In spite of his Protestant zeal he held high office under both Mary and Lady Jane Grey, but he died at his house in Blackfriars in 1558 on the day Elizabeth was crowned Queen of England. His body was taken up the Thames by barge, and he was the first of the Hoby line to be buried in Bisham Abbey. His body was taken much later to the church nearby where, together with his half-brother Sir Thomas who succeeded him, he now lies buried next to the even more splendid tomb of later Hobys which, covered with coats-of-arms of all their allied families, is heraldically one of the finest in England.

This Sir Thomas had been custodian and host to the young Princess Elizabeth when she was virtually held as a prisoner at Bisham by Queen Mary, and he it was who married the woman who has haunted the abbey ever since in her grim and sinister manner. Sir Thomas was only thirty-six years old and ambassador to the French court when he died in Paris. His wife who had accompanied him, was again pregnant and overwhelmed with grief at her sudden loss. Once more a Hoby body had to be brought back to Bisham but this time she determined to have the most beautiful tomb money could buy 'to enclose two such worthy knights' as she called them in their epitaph.

Lady Hoby herself had been as much in favour with Queen Elizabeth as her husband, for she had acted as governess to the princess at Bisham and had quite probably met Sir Thomas there. She was an outstandingly brilliant woman, a great Greek and Latin scholar, speaking and writing both languages with remarkable fluency, and able to write elegies and epitaphs for all her friends. Her two sons, both her daughters, and her three sisters were all highly gifted intellectually, so that the sudden appearance and unsolved mystery of a child named William is wholly inexplicable, even more because of his stupidity and carelessness, which Lady Hoby was the very last person in the world to tolerate. She became more and more exasperated, writing about him to her brother-in-law, Lord Burghley, in very strong language. The boy not only had a hearty dislike of the lessons she set him but lacked the ability to do them, adding slovenliness and carelessness to anger her still more. She began to thrash him every time he failed to do his homework, and if he managed to do it she flogged him again because it was always badly or wrongly done. The tension between them grew and the whippings increased. There came a day, inevitably, when his work was such a slovenly mess, his copy-book so covered with blots and erasures, that she gave him a more than usually savage beating before shutting him up in a small closet with his copy-books to do all over again. There she left him to go to Windsor where the Queen had earlier summoned her. She said nothing to the servants about the punishment of the boy. When she returned she asked the servants where the boy was but remembering she had not told them, she went to the closet and found the child lying dead, his copy-books beside him.

In the year 1840 workmen doing repairs to the abbey discovered a small room where, between the floor joists, they found a pile of copy-books bearing the name of William Hoby. One of these showed Elizabethan characters penned in a childish hand and almost totally illegible with smudges and tears. By the next day the books had most mysteriously disappeared.

Long before this (231 years after her death in 1609) Lady Hoby's ghost began to haunt the abbey. She is always seen gliding rather than walking, a basin floating before her without any visible means of support, in which she continuously washes her guilty hands of the blood she caused to be spilt. It strikes absolute terror into those who have seen it.

There is no mystery about this ghost, but there is a very real mystery about the boy who was beaten to death so savagely. By her second marriage to Lord John Russell, two days before Christmas 1574 and eight years after her first husband died, Lady Hoby had only one son named Francis who died in infancy. In none of the Hoby pedigrees does the name William appear, so who was this unknown boy who causes the evil haunting by his supposed mother, who has often been heard bitterly and hysterically sobbing?

One night during the last war, when the abbey was used as a hospital, a night nurse heard this outburst of sobbing, and greatly alarmed went to find out who it was. She made a complete tour of the wards without discovering anything at all. As she herself said, she only realised afterwards that even if someone had been crying in those wards the very thick abbey walls would have prevented her hearing it anyway. Since then others have heard the sobbing.

Once when Lady Kinloch, who had rented Bisham Abbey, brought a house party down from London, she put one of the young guests in a small room. During the night the house was awakened by the terrified screaming of the girl as she stumbled her way downstairs, unable to speak at all for some time. She finally related how she had been first woken by her clock being smashed to fragments in the fireplace, followed by her toilet set being invisibly seized and thrown right across the room. This was and is the only recorded poltergeist incident at Bisham, but could this particular room have been the one where Lady Hoby put the beaten child?

The Vansittarts owned Bisham after the Hoby line died out in 1780, and in yet another room, one night, a guest heard the sound of water dripping constantly. This became so insistent that his dog, a retriever, showed more alarm even than his master, crouching in terror on the ground until in a great bound of fear, he leapt on to the bed, causing his master to faint away for a time. When morning came the dog was still shivering with terror beside him. So perhaps this was the haunted room.

The greatest moment of fear in the abbey must have been the night Admiral George Vansittart himself endured about fifty years ago, and left on permanent record. He was sitting in the library one night after a game of chess with his brother, which had gone on for so long that it was very late indeed when his brother went upstairs to bed. The admiral stayed there alone, 'turning over in my mind the events of the day. I was certainly not thinking of Lady Hoby.' He was looking down the room when quite suddenly he felt there was someone immediately behind him, and turning in alarm he was appalled to see Lady Hoby herself standing there. His eyes automatically focussed on the wall where her portrait usually hung. The frame was still there but to his horror he saw that it was empty. In terror he got up and rushed from the room, incoherent with fear and incredulity.

The Vansittart family itself had its problems, for no male succeeded in the direct line, the son always predeceasing the father. The family believed that this was due to the curse put upon all owners of Bisham by the last abbot when his abbey was dissolved, though the curse seemed to have by-passed the Hobys.

Lady Hoby herself died and was buried in Bisham church on 2 June 1609. Lord John Russell had died before her and was buried in Westminster Abbey, his epitaph being written by her. She had, while on her deathbed, already designed her own magnificent funeral monument, showing her kneeling at a desk, a coronet on her widow's coif. Facing her is her only surviving daughter Anne, also wearing a coronet and a peeress's robes; three deceased daughters and two surviving sons also kneel there as well as the small swaddled bundle representing Francis Russell, who died as an infant. It is a rich and splendid monumental tomb, enclosed within great iron palisades, covered with heraldry and bearing her own massive epitaph in Latin and English.

Lady Hoby's last action was to write to Sir William Dethick, at that time Garter King of Arms, desiring to know what number of mourners were due to her, the manner of the hearse, the heralds, and the church. Can this really be the woman who murdered that unhappy child? Why was his skeleton not with his copy-books, and why did they disappear the very day after the discovery by the workmen? It would have been quite easy in the sixteenth century to have disposed of an unwanted child, but usually a skeleton has finally appeared, even centuries later. But in the case of the boy William, Hoby or not, there has been no evidence whatsoever even of his existence. Perhaps after nearly four centuries it is not Lady Hoby's ghost at all. But then why should she appear so like her portrait, according to all who have seen her; and why, on that terrifying night in the library, did she step from her frame on the wall?

The more one tries to reason it all out the harder it becomes, but whoever the ghost is it is still very much there, an unquiet, lonely, uncommunicative, guilty ghost, forever washing the blood from its hands and bringing terror to all who have encountered it and felt the sense of evil it brings with it. It is all very strange and mysterious, exactly as all ghost stories should be.

BUCKLEBURY

The unhappy Lady Bolingbroke

It is difficult to imagine that any ghosts could disturb the serene peace of this beautiful Berkshire village between Newbury and Reading, through which the little River Pang flows. The pretty glebe cottages huddle together near the fine Norman church behind them, and acres of fields, meadows and common land surround the village. Here during the momentous battles of Newbury in the Civil War, the Parliamentary troops encamped. Its common, about five miles long, contains over 250 tracks leading in all directions, petering out and joining up again, filtering their intricate ways through high bracken, gorse and shining silver birches.

From Wood Gate in the east a magnificent mile-long avenue of splendid oaks begins, said to have been planted in the reign of Queen Anne by Viscount Bolingbroke to commemorate the victories of Marlborough in France. There is no concrete evidence for this, and judging by the wholesale massacre of trees he caused when he returned from his flight to France, it seems extremely unlikely that it was Bolingbroke who planted them. But along the great avenue of oaks and in the village itself, one ghost moved frequently, causing great fear during its many appearances in the village. A funeral cortège of four bearers all dressed in white would appear, moving together in dead silence and carrying a shrouded corpse on a kind of stretcher. It usually passed through at about midnight when the church clock above the cottages began to strike the hour. It caused such increasing fear whenever it was seen or heard by watching and listening villagers, who dared not sleep if it was a bright moonlight night when the ghostly procession most often passed through the village, that one day some of the younger people plucked up sufficient courage to do something about it.

They encouraged one of their number, either by taunts, threats or intimidation, to lie in wait for the procession on the next moonlight night. The appointed boy hid himself in the churchyard, not in itself the best place to test one's courage, and lay in wait. Sure enough, as the clock began to strike midnight, he saw the four white figures approaching, moving down the road on which the boy himself was now standing apprehensively, hidden by a tree, listening to the eerie pattering and shuffling of the feet of the four bearers. As they drew nearer he plainly saw that they were carrying a corpse on what looked like a stretcher.

With a yell, and brandishing a heavy club, he sprang from his hiding place, rushing towards the ghosts; but swiftly, suddenly, silently, they dropped their load and vanished in four different directions. On the road lay the corpse, covered in its white sheet. It must have taken great courage for the boy to move at all, much less finally to draw near, pull away the shroud and reveal the dead body, but he eventually did so. There, to his astonishment and delight at having forever destroyed the ghostly legend, he saw a dead sheep. These were the days of body-snatching and sheep stealing, the punishment for the latter being death by hanging, or trans- portation. It was no wonder therefore, that the ghostly bearers silently disappeared and never haunted the village again.

There was another ghost which not even that boy dared to disprove, and which caused the terrified villagers to keep their doors and windows tightly locked against its dreaded appearance. This ghost has never been laid, and has been frequently seen in the past, though not recently. It has been observed coming along the great avenue of oaks leading to the manor house near the village, or entering or leaving the entrance to it, passing at dead of night through the village and suddenly vanishing, often being seen approaching or leaving the manor house. This spectre consists of a carriage drawn by six black horses, on the leading one of which sits a headless postillion. Inside the carriage sits a woman dressed all in white; sometimes she is weeping, hiding her bowed head in her hands; sometimes she just stares straight ahead, perfectly motionless. There has never been any doubt that this is the ghost of the unhappy Lady Bolingbroke, who, in the eighteenth century, lived in the manor house, her rightful property by descent, with her brilliant but infamous husband Viscount Bolingbroke, Secretary of State to Queen Anne.

It may be that the stories of this ghostly coach and horses sprang from the clause in her will that stated: 'I desire to be buried in the chancel of Bucklebury church, and to be carried there from the place where I happen to die in a hearse adorned as is usual for persons of my quality attended only with three coaches and six horses to each coach.' Buried in the chancel she certainly is, a slab on the floor bearing the words: 'Here lyeth the Body of Frances Lady Viscountess Bolingbroke Daughter of Sir Henry Winchcombe Bart., who departed this life the 24 day of October AD 1718 Aet 39.' Surely there must be peace at last for her here in this beautiful church, with its Royal Arms, its six splendid funeral hatchments, Georgian box pews, pulpit with sounding board, and fine Brangwyn east window depicting the Crucifixion. Yet it has been recorded that her ghost has even been seen here, though long ago, and perhaps before her 'dear lord' died.

The village of Bucklebury once belonged to Reading Abbey, the manor house becoming the property of John

Winchcombe, son of the celebrated Jack o' Newbury, at the Dissolution of the Monasteries by Henry VIII. In 1550 Winchcombe built a splendid manor house there, his descendants continuing to live in it and control the vast estates until 1830, when the greater part of it was demolished by fire. The only portions left were the huge kitchen fireplace, the brewhouses, the stables bearing the date 1626, and the famous fish-ponds.

The Winchcombe family held the estate for less than 200 years, and in 1703, when the second Sir Henry Winchcombe died leaving no male issue, the estate devolved upon his daughters and co-heiresses, Frances, Elizabeth and Mary. Two years before her father's death Frances, the beautiful eldest daughter, then aged twenty-two, had married Henry St John, Viscount Bolingbroke, Secretary of State to Queen Anne and this tiny Berkshire village became, in its own small way, an important political centre.

Bolingbroke's life up to the time of his marriage had been anything but blameless, for he found women irresistible and his many affairs with them were passionate and short. According to one of his biographers: 'he had an extraordinary ability to sit everyone out at drink, often enough lasting throughout the night, drinking unlimited quantities of his celebrated champagnes and burgundies specially imported to his cellars. In his worst moments he cursed, twaddled, quarrelled, and even blurted out state secrets.' His young wife however, attracted by this dashing and dedicated rake, fondly imagined she alone could manage and even reform him. But although she forgave him again and again to the very end of her life, she never succeeded in altering one single part of his mercurial character. Macaulay, with his usual pungency, trenchantly wrote of him as 'this brilliant knave', an astonishingly accurate summing-up of the man's character.

After their marriage in London they came to live in the splendid Tudor manor house, which Lady Bolingbroke had inherited together with a substantial fortune as dowry. Here, with his beautiful lady, whose heart he finally broke, whose estates and personal fortune he squandered, and whom he eventually completely abandoned, Bolingbroke settled temporarily. For a short time at least he forsook his outrageously licentious life in London and at the Court. His deep drinking, incessant gambling, and the constant masterly intriguing which toppled so many of his opponents like ninepins, prevented him from ever settling down for long to the rustic life which he thought he might be able to enjoy.

Bolingbroke enthusiastically and impetuously set up an extravagant establishment at Bucklebury, befitting a man of his high position and reputation. During the rest of his short and hectic career in England he loved to escape to the peace and quiet of this little village to recover from his busy affairs of state and his perpetual drinking. He travelled often in his splendid coach between Bucklebury and his magnificent London house in Golden Square. He arranged for a French dancing-master to be kept at the manor house for 'Dice', as he fondly called his wife. There was a resident clocksmith to keep his great collection of clocks and watches in time, and a chef whose life was made miserable if he made a mistake serious enough to send Bolingbroke into one of his dangerous tempers, paranoic in their paroxysms. There was also a brewer, a steward, a secretary, and a large staff of servants, grooms, gardeners and farm labourers. The cellars were filled with the choicest wines and spirits sent down specially from his London wine merchants. His stables were filled with fine horses, his kitchens with choice dishes, his fish-ponds stocked with trout and carp. He had hosts of friends and plenty of money.

Here then he could entertain his guests and friends with lavish hospitality. Harley, Parnell, Prior, Pope, Gay, Arbuthnot and Dean Swift, author of *Gulliver's Travels*, were often here. Swift came more frequently than any for he was one of Bolingbroke's closest friends and advisers, and even preached in the village church. There must have been endless hours of drinking and immortal, unrecorded talk by the fish-ponds, Bolingbroke's favourite spot, where he sat with friends, or with his wife, or simply alone.

For thirteen years he came and went here, dividing his life between being lord of the manor of Bucklebury and Secretary of State to Queen Anne in London. Towards the end he was drinking heavily, and boasted that after drinking all night he had still managed to open and close no less than eight field-gates on his way home. The drinking and gambling sessions went on far into the night; his exhausted wife finally went to bed, leaving him with cronies who took all he offered them and more. Dr Stratford, a friend of them both and rector of Little Shefford, a nearby village, wrote to Lord Harley, whose quarrel with Bolingbroke Swift had tried in vain to heal: 'I went last week to pay a visit to a poor disconsolate ladye in Berkshire. I met nothing there but sorrow and disorder.'

The clouds were indeed gathering over Lady Bolingbroke and she had nothing left but her love and unswerving loyalty towards her worthless husband, constantly concerned about his welfare. She even went to London to pay his massive gambling debts. The final crushing blow came when she discovered that 'her dear lord' had taken for his mistress a French woman, the Marquise Villette, with whom he really seemed to be in love, and upon whom he lavished money and gifts. It was this which finally broke Lady Bolingbroke's heart.

Yet in Viscount Bolingbroke's sudden fall from power at

the hands of George I, swifter than any he had brought to his enemies, his wife was the first to rally to his side when all had deserted him except Swift and the marquise; but it was in vain, for he turned away from her to his new love. His political career was in ruins, for he had made an implacable enemy of Walpole. He was attainted under George I for all his actions and conduct under Queen Anne, dismissed from all his offices and stripped of all his honours, titles and estates. Before he could be arrested he fled to France to live with his mistress in her country and to offer his services to the Old Pretender, who gladly received him.

On 27 October 1718 Dr Stratford wrote his last letter from Bucklebury to Lord Harley: 'I know not whether I shall be the first that gives you notice of poor Lady Bolingbroke's death. She died on Friday morning about eight o'clock. When the will was opened it appeared she had given all that was left to herself and had not been given to her husband at his leaving England to her godson.'

When Bolingbroke was informed of his wife's death he betrayed no emotion at all, but was furious over the will which had completely omitted him. When he was told also that she died in great piety he was heard to say to the marquise: 'What a supple thing religion is and how it sanctifies everything especially when managed by a skilful director.' Two years later he married his mistress.

It is round the extensive fish-ponds that Lady Bolingbroke's ghost has most often been seen, for here some of the most famous people of the day, guests of her husband and herself, would sit and talk the hours away. Her ghost would move round and round, restlessly wringing her hands, her head bowed, often weeping as she did when riding in the coach, but more often just sitting where her husband used to sit, waiting expectantly for his return.

There are still two other places haunted by the restless

ghost of this wronged and unhappy lady, both of them secret passages leading from the cellars of the manor house itself. One was the escape route used by Bolingbroke when the net was closing in on him and he made his flight to France. The other is connected with the former vicarage, on the site of which now stands a fine Georgian house with a garden open to the public every year. Here her spirit wanders first in one direction, then another, in a constant search for her lord. As for the fine avenue of oaks reputed to be planted by him, there is a bitter comment in yet another of Dr Stratford's letters after Bolingbroke had returned to England:

> Bolingbroke is come to town and has signalised his return by a very dishonourable action. He has made strange havoc at Bucklebury, he has cut down all the trees in the grove and about the house that was a defence as well as an ornament to it. He has cleared all the hedges round the estate, he has marked 1,100 trees to be cut that are so small as not to be valued at half-a-crown apiece. In short he seems resolved to ruin that estate to the utmost of his power.

It is as well that Lady Bolingbroke lies at last in peace in that beautiful church, with the sun pouring down on her through the splendid Brangwyn east window. How delighted she would have been to know that her present descendant, Mr Hartley Russell, has quite recently re-stocked the fishponds she loved so much and so often sat beside.

But there is one inexplicable thing in the whole of this story. Who was the headless postillion seated on the leader of the six horses drawing the ghostly coach in which she is seen riding? Could he have been a victim of one of his master's paranoic outbursts of drunken rage? We shall never know. Bolingbroke's ghost at least has never been seen in Bucklebury and perhaps it is just as well for he caused enough sorrow and distraction there in his lifetime.

CUMNOR HALL

Amy Robsart

The news of Amy Robsart's tragic and mysterious death on Sunday, 8 September 1560 not only shocked England but half Europe as well. Rumours flashed from lip to lip, from country to country; ambassadors reported hurriedly to their princes and sovereigns. All waited expectantly for the next move on the political chessboard, and none more than Philip of Spain. Was it accidental death, or suicide, or even murder? What would her husband, the rakish, dashing Robert Dudley, later Earl of Leicester, the leading favourite and, some whispered, even the lover of Queen Elizabeth, do now?

For eight years after her marriage Amy Robsart, daughter of Sir John Robsart of Norfolk, had lived in Lincolnshire. She and her husband had then gone to Berkshire staying with their friends, the Hydes of Denchworth, before moving in to Cumnor Hall, where Anthony Forster was steward, household treasurer and personal friend of Robert Dudley. On that fatal night a fair was being held at nearby Abingdon, where Amy gave her staff permission to go and enjoy themselves; indeed, she actually urged them to go. When they had all gone, according to evidence later given at the trial, she sat down to play at tables with three lady friends. One of them, Mrs Owen, a widow and sister of Amy's friend Mrs Hyde, stayed on alone to dine with Amy before going home herself. When the staff returned late that night the house was still and quiet, a sense of doom over it. This was proved almost at once when they found the body of their young and beautiful mistress lying at the bottom of the wide staircase.

Her neck was broken and showed unmistakable signs of strangulation. Her face was badly bruised, and her lips were blue with the poison which had obviously been forced between them.

Almost at once her ghost began to haunt the house, the gardens, the courtyard, but most of all the staircase, so that none of her servants dared go up to their rooms. For over 300 years her ghost has appeared, not only there but as far away as Kenilworth. As the years passed tenants came and went, never staying long, driven out by the terrifying screams of a woman, and the sight of her ghost appearing at all hours of the day and night. Attempts were made to exorcise it finally by the customary nine priests who came from Oxford. They tried to lay Amy's restless and unhappy spirit to rest forever in a pond, known since as Lady Dudley's pond. It is said that never afterwards did the pond freeze, but the exorcism did nothing to allay her ghost. In 1814, being no longer inhabitable, the house was demolished, many of its stones being taken away by the fifth Earl of Abingdon to rebuild Wytham Church. But still her ghost flits among the ruins and has been seen comparatively recently.

Mickle, a poet of the latter half of the eighteenth century, composed a ballad on her tragic death:

> Sore and sad that lady grieved
> In Cumnor Hall, so lone and drear;
> Full many a piercing scream was heard
> And many a cry of mortal fear.
>
> The death knell thrice was heard to ring,
> An aerial voice was heard to call;
> And thrice the raven flapped its wing
> Around the towers of Cumnor Hall.
>
> And in that manor now no more
> Is cheerful feast and sprightly ball:
> For ever since that dreary hour
> Have spirits haunted Cumnor Hall.

The village maids with fearful glance
Avoid the ancient moss-grown wall,
Nor ever lead the sprightly dance
Among the groves of Cumnor Hall.

All that now remains of Cumnor Hall is close to the church, almost a part of it; fragments of wall and the open fireplace of the once splendid mansion in which Amy Robsart died. Here her spirit now moves and has often been seen, perhaps restlessly seeking the long-vanished staircase at the foot of which she was found dead on that Sunday night over 300 years ago.

To judge from extant letters at Longleat, home of the Marquis of Bath, and in Cumnor Church vestry itself, she and her husband were reasonably happy, for she wrote graciously and affectionately of and to 'my dear lord'. She dealt with the estate, with the help of Anthony Forster, who beside being the steward was the MP for Abingdon, showing her skill and attention for the care of the property, the sale of sheep and wool, and the well-being of the servants. Throughout her husband's long and frequent absences at Court, Amy was accustomed to being often alone, never suspecting that there were far more cogent reasons for her husband's being so often with the Queen. The Spanish ambassador was already writing of Dudley's 'over preposterous pretentions' and, more warningly, 'should something untoward happen for the king that is to be'. Inevitably the gossip spread from London across the country and finally to Cumnor, where a stunned and unhappy Amy first heard the whispers that were so swiftly to lead to her death. If she knew nothing of what a contemporary writer described as Dudley's 'peacock personality', she must surely have known of his extravagance and gluttony, his love of fine clothes, his courtly manners, his handsome features, and the skill at dancing which first endeared him to the Queen. Of his ruthlessness, cruelty, uncontrollable ambition and lechery, she perhaps knew nothing, or kept what she knew to herself, but she grew more and more unhappy and apprehensive of something she could not understand.

Dudley's own household books during this time however, and on his infrequent visits to Cumnor Hall, seemed concise and agreeable enough, describing visits to the estate farms, to friends and local people. His restless spirit and love for his queen, the most glittering star in his firmament, soon drove him back to Court again. Amy herself, by virtue of her own descent and now high rank, was quite well aware of the intrigues and subtleties of life at Court, but it was not until after her death that Mrs Pinto, her personal maid, revealed how many times she had seen her mistress weep and 'pray to God to deliver her from her desperation'. Indeed, it was this very statement which led many people to believe that she committed suicide, though it is hardly feasible that she would have done this unless she had absolute evidence of her husband's infidelity.

Once again the Spanish ambassador, collecting gossip as busily as a bee does honey, reported the first evidence of what was to come, writing: 'The Queen and Dudley have given out that Amy Robsart is ill, but she is, in fact, very well indeed, though taking great steps not to be poisoned.' This was a very significant and dangerous statement indeed from anyone, more so from an ambassador. Later he wrote: 'Dudley has more than once most indiscreetly spoken of getting Amy out of the way as both he and the Queen are acknowledged lovers.' None of this was acceptable to his master, Phillip II, who had planned to marry the Archduke Charles to Queen Elizabeth. Yet rumours and gossip continued to come from his ambassador to the Escorial. This time he claimed that Dudley and the Queen were secretly married, and that a woman had been sent to prison not only for saying so but for adding 'that the Queen was now with child by Dudley'.

But the two most incomprehensible things about the whole of this tragic affair come from Dudley himself. He was at Windsor when the news of his wife's death was brought to him by express messenger. Instead of going himself to Cumnor, he sent his cousin Sir Thomas Blount to investigate and report the whole matter to him. Even more incredible was his absence from her funeral, and these two facts did nothing at all to allay fast-growing suspicions that he had had her murdered. Dudley ordered his wife's body to be brought from Cumnor to Worcester College, Oxford, and thence in costly and solemn procession to St Mary's Church for interment with lavish pomp and ceremony, attended by the University and City authorities, officers of the College of Arms, and many other high Court officials. The full expense was £2,000, an immense sum of money in those times.

All Sir Thomas Blount's efforts to find out the truth about Amy Robsart's death were fruitless, and he encountered only a wall of silent suspicion, hostility and fear from all the neighbouring gentry. They were all too well aware of the cause of death but such was the immense power of Dudley that they kept their opinions to themselves, beginning to seek secret methods of inquiry into the whole ugly business. Lord Burghley himself, when presenting to the Queen his reasons why she should not marry Dudley, if that was her intention, now stated 'that he is infamed by the death of his wife'. Elizabeth, when vexed, either flew into a rage or remained silent. This time she chose the latter course.

Meanwhile fresh rumours were circulating at Abingdon that on the night of Amy's death Anthony Forster and another conspirator had remained concealed in Cumnor Hall until all the staff, and later Amy's friends, had left. They had then seized Amy, trying and failing to poison her by force, strangled her and flung her headlong down the stairs to make it look like suicide or an accident. It was still further asserted that to prevent any unfavourable details becoming public Dudley had given orders to have Anthony Forster strangled, and this was carried out. Amy's own half-brother, John Appleyard, when questioned by Sir Thomas Blount, spoke vaguely of 'this great misfortune which had taken place in the house of Master Forster whose honesty did much curb the evil thoughts of the people'. It was not until seven years later, when he was summoned by the Privy Council, then debating the whole question of Dudley's part in his wife's suspected murder, that Appleyard made a significant statement which he had not dared to utter before. 'While I do not hold Dudley guilty I think it would not be difficult to find out the guilty parties.' If, as would seem, this was some retraction of his earlier statement, it could well have been made under pressure.

One thing is absolutely certain, and that is that all records of the coroner's inquest, and the report on the death of Amy Robsart, have completely disappeared. The trial itself seems to have been a complete farce, for both Dudley and Blount were in the closest communication with the jury. It was even said that Dudley actually bribed the foreman without even Blount's knowledge, to make absolutely certain of the verdict, thus leaving Blount to intimidate or bribe them. Dudley meanwhile openly urged them to speak the truth, the whole truth and nothing but the truth. Lady Warwick's correspondence at the time of the trial speaks tellingly of the jury, saying 'he, Dudley, doth protest too much', and adds extracts which prove beyond question that both he and Blount were in the closest communication with the jury before, during, and after the trial. It was no surprise to all who sat in court, when the jury returned a verdict of not guilty, 'for after a most searching enquiry they could find no presumption of evil doing'.

The Queen's relationship with Dudley now became even closer. Once again rumours were rife, suggesting that she had not only been secretly married in Lord Pembroke's house, 'but was a mother already'. In spite of their closer intimacy however, Elizabeth was never a woman completely to lose control of her political life and actions, which Dudley was now endeavouring to influence. His actions led to fierce rebukes and open quarrels. When he tried to have Black Rod dismissed from office for instance he incurred her fullest wrath, which even he dared not defy. Still she made no move to marry him.

Some years after Amy's death Dudley secretly married the daughter of Lord Howard of Effingham, and when Elizabeth was informed of this by her spies she was beside herself with fury. Once again, because of his attempt to poison his second wife, the ugly rumours began to circulate, ballads and lampoons changing hands as fast as they were composed. Finally one of them renewed the charge of murder against Dudley of his first wife Amy Robsart. Fresh evidence revealed that before Amy's death messengers had been sent to Dr Bayley, a famous professor of physic at Oxford, to obtain a potion for her. The doctor had however, refused to prescribe one 'knowing her to be perfectly well at the time and that if they poisoned her under the name of his potion he might be hanged for a cover for their sin'.

Still nothing happened to Dudley, but when a few years later he made a third secret marriage to Lettice Knollys the Queen's anger was terrifying. She commanded Dudley to come at once and, after passionately and angrily upbraiding him, suddenly gave him a stinging slap on the face and ordered him from Court, viciously threatening 'to throw both himself and that she-wolf his wife in the Tower'. It was the beginning of the end for Dudley. After this virtual dismissal from her presence and from the Court life he had lived and loved for so long, Dudley had no influence whatsoever over the Queen, much less so since his disastrous failure as governor of the Netherlands, which she had earlier appointed him.

The last year of his life was uneventful; his health not being good he set out for Kenilworth, disconsolate and disillusioned. On the way he stopped at Rycote House to write his last letter to the Queen, then proceeded on his way to Cornbury Park. There, while hunting one day in Wychwood Forest, he came face to face with the ghost of Amy Robsart. True to the legend she solemnly warned him of his imminent death and that he would soon be joining her once again. Anxious, frightened, drained of all his reserves, he returned to the house where he was lodging. Five days later he was dead.

He was buried in the collegiate church of Warwick, his funeral costing £4,000, double the sum he spent on Amy Robsart's. Ben Jonson tells the story that Dudley had given his wife 'a bottle of liquor which he willed her to use in any faintness, and which she, not knowing it was poison, gave him, and so he died'. It is irony indeed if the story is true. Dudley was mourned by few in England, least of all by his third wife, who almost immediately married her lover, Christopher Blount, Gentleman of the Horse to her dead husband. It was even rumoured that she herself gave Dudley 'a poisoned cordial after a heavy meal', but proof of this has never been established. The Queen expressed her sorrow in a very strange way. 'His death,' says Rapin, 'drew tears from the queen, who, nevertheless, ordered his goods to be sold at public sale for payment of the sums she had lent him.'

Perhaps the most pathetic relics of the whole tragic story

31

are to be found in Cumnor Church vestry. There, close to the splendid stone statue of Queen Elizabeth which had once been put by Dudley in the gardens of Cumnor Hall, are facsimile letters of both Amy and her lord, a portrait showing how beautiful she was, and detailed bills from her London tailor, two of which arrived after her death. At the other end of the church, in the chancel itself, is the tomb of Anthony Forster, the supposed murderer, and his wife. Here are all the principal actors in this unsolved drama, as near to each other in death as in life.

Throughout the years since Amy's death Cumnor Hall remained empty, gradually deteriorating, for none would live there, so haunted and so full of evil was the place. The legend grew that whoever saw her ghost would shortly after die. This fear was enough to keep people away, and only owls and bats lived there, and 'the flapping of the raven's wings', of which the poet Mickle wrote, could still be heard. To the west of the church are the broken walls, the open fireplace, the great empty space where once stood the splendid house and where now the grass and weeds grow. A lasting sadness and indefinable uneasiness seemed to be over it all. Perhaps the unhappy, restless ghost of Amy Robsart was there at that moment as the pale sun broke through the clouds. It was time to go.

HURLEY

The wilful monks of Ladye Place

Even if we had not been going to Hurley, the intriguingly imperative signpost would have sent us. 'Hurley only' it starkly said, as if beyond that there was only uninhabited space. So we turned off the noisy, dreary London–Maidenhead–Henley road and followed the sign to one of the most charming of Berkshire villages.

There it all was; the sixteenth-century picture-book inn, the Norman, originally Saxon church, the medieval tithebarn and the splendid, circular dovecote; and beyond, blocking it all off, ran the Thames. It was indeed Hurley only, for the one way in was the one way out, and sandwiched between that dreary road and the lovely river was a place of peace and harmony which could not have changed very much since the year 1086 when Geoffrey de Mandeville first founded a Benedictine priory there.

This Geoffrey de Mandeville came over with William the Conqueror and was rewarded by vast estates and lands in many English counties, as well as the first chartered earldom of Essex. He was one of the most arrogant, cruel and bloodthirsty anarchists in English history. He looted, pillaged, burned and raped his way up and down the country, first fighting for Stephen then for Maud, then back again to Stephen, and once again for Maud, exacting each time higher and richer rewards, titles and castles, until his name was feared throughout England, finally causing the barons to unite to drive him out.

Almost as soon as Hurley Priory was founded, the Bene-

dictine monks set to work to build, first enlarging the existing church; the exceedingly beautiful Norman west door is
evidence even today of the high quality of their architectural
skill. Still existing also, apart from the tithe-barn and dovecote, are the cloister court of the monastery on the north
side of the church, and the refectory or dining hall. On the
site of this priory, in Elizabethan times, a magnificent house
was built called Ladye Place after the patron saint of the
church, the Blessed Virgin Mary. It is said to have been
haunted ever since by the Grey Lady, though only in legend,
for no one ever seems to have seen her, or if so has left no
record of what he saw.

Ladye Place was built by Sir Richard Lovelace in 1558
'out of money gotten with Sir Francis Drake'. Fuller, in his
Worthies of England writes that Sir Richard 'was a gentleman of metal, and in the reign of Queen Elizabeth, making
use of letters of mart, had the success to light on a large
remnant of the King of Spain's cloth of silver, I mean his
West Indian fleet, wherewith he and his posterity are the
warmer to this day.' Sir Richard was created Baron Lovelace
of Hurley, the title becoming extinct in 1736.

When writing of John, Lord Lovelace, a descendant of
Sir Richard, Macaulay says 'in the dark chambers below
this mansion some zealous and daring opponents of the
government held many midnight conferences during that
anxious time when England was impatiently awaiting the
Protestant wind.' This refers to William of Orange, whom
the Whig peers determined to invite to England as king and
thus overthrow the Catholic James II they hated so much.
The plot was headed by John, Lord Lovelace, who was
appointed captain of the band of gentlemen petitioners to
the prince. All the conferences were held in the crypt of
Ladye Place, to which William later came when he was king,
being magnificently entertained by Lord Lovelace in the

mansion above. Lovelace's great prodigality and splendid style of living, however, became so excessive that he was forced to sell part of his estate to pay his steeply mounting debts.

This crypt was undoubtedly part of the former abbey, and had at one time been the monks' burial place. This was borne out when the house was demolished in 1838 and the bodies of three monks in the robes of the Benedictine order were found. Henry VIII had ordered the monks to be driven out and their monastery to be ransacked for its treasures, after which the whole place fell into rack and ruin.

In 1924, the house, now rebuilt in Edwardian style, was inhabited by a Colonel Rivers-Moore. He bought Ladye Place with its twenty acres of surrounding land, for he was an archaeologist and firmly convinced that it contained somewhere the coffin of Editha, sister of Edward the Confessor, who was reputed to have been buried there by him in the Saxon church. The colonel believed with equal conviction that the Grey Lady who, legend had it, haunted the place, was Editha's ghost although he had never at any time seen the legendary Grey Lady. Neither he nor anyone else in that peaceful village could have foreseen the disturbances and upheavals which arose from almost the first days of his thoroughly planned system of excavations to find the coffin. The Grey Lady ceased to exist but the Benedictine monks took over in no small way.

The first evidence the colonel had of their existence was the sudden apparition of a monk in a brown habit of the Benedictine order. It indicated by ghostly gestures and signs that there existed a fireplace in the house which the colonel was to excavate, and then vanished. The next day the puzzled but deeply interested colonel saw him again in another room where he rightly considered the fireplace to be. Again, after making signs of digging, the figure disappeared. The colonel at once began excavations, and discovered not only the new fireplace but behind it an even larger one belonging to the original priory.

Such a preliminary discovery further confirmed the colonel's belief that he would eventually reveal the mystery of the Grey Lady and he and his team redoubled their efforts. The monk who had first guided him never returned, but some weeks later in another part of the house where he was working, a second monk appeared, also in the habit of the Benedictine order, even more anxious it seemed, to guide the colonel. In some strange way, the colonel received messages that the monk's name was King, and that some four centuries earlier he had stolen a small casket of jewels which he had thrown into a well for safety and in the hope of recovery. The ghostly monk then vanished.

Once again the colonel switched from his main plan of excavation, and after some time found the well. That same night the monk returned, strangely excited and very restless. Next day one of the team 'sensed' a presence he could not see, but one which seemed to be encouraging them in their work. The colonel began the task of clearing the rubble of four centuries from the deep well, and after days of digging found at the very bottom a casket containing a small quantity of medieval jewellery. The monk appeared once more that same night now gratified and at peace. He was never seen again, but others followed, and quite soon too.

The colonel was now utterly convinced Ladye Place would reveal Editha's tomb, and for the next twenty-three years he became totally obsessed with his quest, determined to find it somewhere in that former splendid Elizabethan mansion. As the crypt had once been the monks' burial place, the colonel reasoned that it was the next place to excavate to the full and so his team of friends and guests set to work in earnest. More strange things began to happen, alarming not only the helpers but as rumours spread, the whole peaceful village. Out of their centuries-old home more monks began to appear.

Possibly the driving motive behind the colonel's excavations derived from a document drawn up during the reign of Richard II which had been buried in the old priory. This is said to have contained much of the valuable evidence supporting the colonel's belief in the location of Editha's tomb in the house. It seems from subsequent appearances of the monks that they sought either to mislead or completely discourage the colonel in his costly task.

During the early days of the new excavations the colonel's brother-in-law, a doctor, came to stay with him. His visit was made with both curiosity and interest as to the colonel's activities. It was obvious that when he came down to breakfast one morning he was badly shaken. When questioned by the colonel he answered that he had seen a ghost, and that it was not the legendary Grey Lady everyone spoke of, but a monk dressed in a long brown Benedictine habit. Whatever the colonel may have thought he kept it to himself. Only a few days later another badly shaken guest reported that he also had seen a similar ghost of a Benedictine monk. As if that were not enough, a third guest repeated the same story a few days later. So disturbed was she by her experience she insisted that the colonel should call in a psychic expert. He did nothing however, and continued with his excavations. There were still more hauntings and visitations, and every ghost was of a monk, the most frequent to appear being one who walked up and down with folded arms. At last the colonel felt compelled to do something about it and got in touch with a medium who came to the house to hold a seance to consult the monks themselves. They could perhaps explain what was troubling them so much that they should come out of hiding after so many centuries, and would perhaps guide the colonel to Editha's tomb.

Apparently, the monks did all they could to help. One of them even confessed that he had himself practised black magic during his lifetime. The seances and excavations went on, and the monks continued to come out of hiding. Then most dramatically at one seance, the colonel and his team were told by one of the ghostly monks that if they followed all his instructions they would find the foundations of the original priory. Excitedly obeying directions they excavated part of the grounds, to reveal a hard base surrounded by tiles. It might well have been an ancient Saxon shrine, and did in fact contain human remains, but disappointingly, not those of Editha.

This blow to all the colonel's plans seems finally to have convinced him that the secret of Editha's tomb would remain wherever it was. The ghosts continued to appear but never gave him any further directions. The whole scheme was also becoming increasingly costly, so with great reluctance the colonel had to abandon his life's dream. In 1947 he put Ladye Place up for auction, going first to Wargrave, then to Scotland, where he died in 1965. The house was divided and sold in three lots, though the name of Ladye Place still remains. As soon as the excavations ceased and the frustrated colonel had given in to the monks, the hauntings ceased; none of the monks have ever been seen again, nor for that matter the Grey Lady. So perhaps they have all returned to the peace and quiet from which they were so brutally disturbed, certain now that such a singular series of excavations and seances will no longer trouble them. They may even have considered the whole thing a victory for themselves, as perhaps it was, but where would the Grey Lady go? She could not very well live with all those monks!

WINDSOR CASTLE

Royal and other ghosts

Most castles in England have been associated at some time in their history with legends, ghosts and poltergeists. Windsor Castle is no exception. Indeed, it probably has more ghosts than any other castle in England, or for that matter, Great Britain. There are at least eight ghosts, of which four are royal and two are animals; none of them is evil or even tragic, for curiously enough, nothing tragic has ever occurred in the castle during its long history. Windsor is not only England's largest castle, covering some thirteen acres, but its premier castle, and was used as such first by William the Conqueror and then, between 1165 and 1173, by Henry 11, who put up the first stone buildings. Its position on a motte or raised mound was of great strategic and defensive importance, and allowed it to dominate the Thames valley 100ft below. Its massive Round Tower is a landmark from which, it is said, one can see fifteen counties. The courtesy of successive sovereigns has enabled millions of people to visit its great state apartments, courtyards, cloisters, gardens and great park; and to see the annual and memorable Order of the Garter service in the splendid St George's Chapel.

For 800 years sovereigns have been born and buried here; and each one has added something to the castle. Henry III finished the walls and built three of the towers. Edward I gave it its charter. Edward III built two more towers, and raised the Round Tower and the Norman gateway. Edward IV began and Henry VII completed St George's Chapel. Henry VIII built the great gateway bearing his name. Queen

Elizabeth I built the north terrace and gallery. Charles II restored the state apartments and George IV transformed the former medieval castle into the palace it is today, and increased still more the height of the Round Tower. William IV built the great Waterloo Chamber. Queen Victoria decorated the Albert Memorial Chapel.

It seems, therefore, remarkable there are not even more than the four royal ghosts known and documented. Two of them haunt the Royal Library, which is not open to the public. This library is full of priceless treasures, some 20,000 drawings, including an unrivalled collection of Leonardo da Vinci's work, drawings by Michelangelo, paintings by Raphael, a Shakespeare with Charles I's autograph, a Caxton printed on vellum, and countless other items. Here, it is said, the ghost of the kindly, mad King George III wanders. He was confined to the castle during the years of his lunacy, where he was badly treated by his keepers. He once broke away from them to chase Fanny Burney round a tree in the Great Park and finally to kiss her. He was so unhappy during his initial imprisonment here that it is no wonder his ghost moves restlessly about the castle. It is said also to haunt Kensington Palace.

A more singular appearance in the Royal Library is the ghost of Queen Elizabeth I, which has been faithfully recorded by Lieutenant Glynn of the Grenadier Guards, stationed in the castle at the time, on the single occasion he saw her. He was sitting one night in the library looking at a book and idly turning its leaves, his mind on nothing in particular and certainly not on ghosts, when he heard the tap-tap of high-heeled shoes as if on an uncarpeted floor. Putting down his book and curious at the sound, he heard the tap-tapping becoming clearer and nearer; looking up he saw to his utter astonishment the tall and stately figure of a woman actually coming towards him from the other end of the library. He instantly recognised her as Queen Elizabeth from a portrait he had seen and the likeness became even more apparent as she drew nearer and passed so close to him that he could have reached out his hand to touch her. Quite spellbound, yet not in any way afraid, he watched her enter an inner room which he knew to have no exit, but as he followed her in she completely disappeared. Elizabeth's ghost was also witnessed at another time by the Empress Frederick of Germany when she was staying in the castle. There could surely be no more astonishing pair of ghosts than this very sane queen and the mad king, and one wonders if they ever meet each other and what are their reactions.

The third royal ghost is of Charles I, who haunts one of the canon's houses and has been identified by his faithful likeness to the portrait Van Dyck painted of him. The fourth is believed to be of Henry VIII, who though he has never been seen has often been heard in the cloisters near the Deanery and in the passages outside. The sounds consist of awful groans and dragging footsteps up and down the gloomy cloister passages, as if the ghostly king were suffering in death from the gout he suffered from in life.

There is also a ghost believed to be that of Sir George Villiers, Duke of Buckingham. In the reign of Charles I one of the king's gentlemen-in-waiting informed him that the duke would very shortly be assassinated, a prophecy which was almost immediately carried out by a Puritan fanatic, to the great joy of the country for he was a much hated man.

The Deanery itself is haunted, and some forty years ago the dean himself recorded hearing someone walking along the passage with three distinct steps which sounded like a woman's. In addition, various residents of the castle have seen the ghost of a woman in grey near the north door of the Deanery. Another witness of the ghostly steps in the

Deanery thought they belonged to a man, and that he took four steps, not three. The dean thought this change might have been due to some alteration in the floor level since the time when he heard the ghost, for there were now three steps by the bathroom door near where the listener slept.

Two other ghostly incidents have occurred in the castle. The first was when a young Grenadier Guards recruit who had seen a ghost in the Long Walk was so terrified that he shot himself. Some weeks later a guardsman, relieving another guard on sentry duty, saw the ghost of this dead guardsman. When he returned from duty to the guardroom, still in terror, he found that the sentry he had relieved had also seen the same ghost, and had been too frightened to tell anyone.

The other incident, also involving a guardsman, was almost as strange, an account of it appearing in the weekly press in 1906. On a grey, misty April morning a sentry in the Coldstream Guards on duty near the east terrace saw the figures of several men coming towards him down the terrace steps. He at once challenged them, and as they still approached did so a second time and yet a third time. He then fired at the leading figure which halted and stood still; he fired again and, fixing his bayonet, prepared to charge, when all the figures mysteriously vanished. It was only then that the realisation came to him that these were spirits. At that moment the castle patrol arrived, alarmed by the shots, but a search of the grounds proved fruitless. For doing his duty so well the sentry, ironically, received three days confined to barracks as a punishment.

The Long Walk of the Great Park is haunted by the famous Herne the Hunter who during the reign of Henry VIII, tradition has it, was warden of Windsor Forest and supposed to practise witchcraft. He was finally found hanging from a branch of a tree known ever since as Herne's Oak, but his ghost appears it is said, whenever disaster threatens the royal family or the nation. He actually appeared to Henry VIII. He is a terrifying ghost, for he wears deerskin clothes, a helmet made from a stag's skull with spreading antlers, and is seen riding a fire-breathing horse accompanied by a pack of hounds. Shakespeare used Herne to good effect in *The Merry Wives of Windsor* to frighten Falstaff.

Not so very long ago two Eton schoolboys were returning to the college one evening through the park, when they heard the distant baying of hounds and the galloping hooves of a horse rushing towards them. Though they actually saw nothing, they were conscious of many feet rushing past them, and of a cold current of air. The spot where Herne's Oak once stood—it was destroyed in 1863—may still be seen on the footpath leading from Windsor road to Queen Adelaide's Lodge in the Little Park, and is haunted by Herne.

The other animal ghost is the White Stag, which has nothing to do with Herne, though it has often been thought of as his quarry when out with his hounds. It is said to appear in the park at times of national importance, and was last seen at the outbreak of World War I.

Such a number of ghosts in a single place seems at first incredible, but no matter how many such incidents have been and still are reported, one must at least give credence to the numerous witnesses who have given evidence and proof of what they have seen of the supernatural world.

A DORSET TRIO

Broadwindsor—The screaming skull of Bettiscombe House

Bettiscombe House stands in the beautiful Marshwood Vale between Lyme Regis and Broadwindsor, six miles north-west of Bridport. Nothing would ever induce the owners of its legendary screaming skull to part with it for fear of unknown disasters, so it remains in its cardboard box for anyone to see who is interested in its history.

Of all the hundreds of ghosts who haunt England's castles, rectories, houses, inns, moors and barns, surely the most evil is that of 'Bloody' Judge Jeffreys, who was closely connected with the screaming skull. His ghost is as terrifying in death as he was in life, according to those who have seen it, even quite recently, in the Great House of Lyme Regis. There he moves about in his scarlet robe, wig and black cap, brandishing a huge and bloody club in his clenched hand. Two of the many hundreds of his victims after the luckless rebellion of Monmouth against James II were the brothers John and Azariah Pinney, sons of the Reverend John Pinney, a Puritan minister holding the living of Broadwindsor, and a well-known lacemaker. They were tried and sentenced to death at Dorchester Assizes. John was executed; Azariah was reprieved but condemned to a life of slavery.

Inconceivable as it sounds, his own sister Hester made a bid for him in the slave auction market, but having secured his freedom she packed him off at once to the West Indies, convinced this hot-headed rebel would be less trouble there than in Dorset and in Bettiscombe House. Azariah went to the island of Nevis where, with the lacemaking skill he had inherited from his father, he began to make and sell his products. He next turned to sugar planting, very soon becoming rich enough to employ his own slaves.

His grandson John Frederick, also a very rich man, decided to return to England and visit the family home, Bettiscombe House, where even today one of the Pinney descendants lives. He brought with him one of his negro slaves and it was then that all the trouble began. The negro hated the damp English air, was no doubt not very well treated by the villagers because of his colour, and pined ceaselessly to return home. Very soon he became ill with consumption and on his deathbed said that his spirit would never rest until his body was returned to his native country. In spite of his last wish he was buried in Bettiscombe churchyard. For some wholly unaccountable reason his skull was kept in one of the attics of the house.

True to his word the negro's spirit began to rebel. Terrifying screams were heard coming from his grave so that no one dared go near the churchyard. At the same time pandemonium broke out in Bettiscombe House; windows rattled, doors banged and slammed at all hours of the day and night and life became intolerable for everyone, both in the house and village. But no one dared remove the skull. William Andrews, in his essay *Skull Superstitions*, states: 'If the skull be brought out of the house the house itself would rock to its foundations, while the perpetrator of such an act of desecration would certainly die within the year.' So it is not at all surprising that the skull is still there in the house. Twice it has been removed and each time, almost immediately, disaster struck.

The first time farm labourers became ill, crops failed and cattle died until the skull was brought back again. The second time a tenant farmer living in the house—it was then a farmhouse—was so angry about the hauntings that one day he picked up the skull and threw it in to the duck-pond outside. The effect was alarming, and immediate. Noises and screaming broke out all over the house, and in the garden and farm buildings. The farmer became even angrier then he was before he threw the skull into the pond. He was forced to empty the pond, and to dig about in the deep mud until he retrieved the skull and brought it back into the house. Only then did the noises stop and so the skull has remained in the house ever since.

Another version of the story has it that the negro's master was not a sugar planter but a priest. The two had a violent quarrel ending in the murder of one of them. It is said the skull screams as it did in its death agony, giving warning of the same fate to those who hear it. Yet another version is that it is not a negroid skull at all, but one from a barrow on the Dorset Downs, screaming a warning of impending death to whoever hears it in the house.

Judge Udal, the leading authority on the Bettiscombe skull, actually believed it to be that of a woman. It has been claimed that the skull belonged to a white woman, a pre-historic man, a fossilised 1,500-year-old white woman, to mention only a few theories; but no one has ever offered any other explanation as to why it screamed or why peace ceases with its removal from the house. It is probably better to leave the skull where it is and to ask no more questions about it.

Beaminster—The daylight ghost

'Drive slowly or break your neck' once warned a notice at the top of the long hill leading down to the charming village of Beaminster, called Emminster by Thomas Hardy in *Tess of the d'Urbervilles*. Six miles from Bridport, it is superbly set amid the open, generous Dorset countryside of lush valleys and chalk hills which end in steep cliffs above the sea. From this peaceful village however, has come one of the most authentic and documented daylight ghost stories in the country as recounted fully in the *Gentleman's Magazine* of 1774.

In May 1728 John Daniel, a twelve-year-old pupil in the church school, suffered badly from fits and had to leave because he was 'ill of the stone'. This did not prevent him from going for walks in the country, which he enjoyed. One day however, he did not return at his usual time and when his anxious mother reported this a search party was sent out. They found the boy's dead body about a furlong from his house and, believing his death had been caused by one of his fits, they buried him in the normal way without any suspicion.

Some seven weeks later, on Saturday 27 June, the master dismissed his class at noon and the boys went into the churchyard to play ball. In those days the school was held in the gallery of the church, which was reached by a flight of steps from the churchyard. After a time four of the boys, one of whom had the classroom key, went back to search for some old pens. As they entered the school they were startled to hear a sound like the booming of a brass pan. At first mystified, then afraid, they began a search of the school but found nothing. They were now badly frightened by the additional noise of a man walking in heavy boots and fled back at once to the others. Their story brought fear to all the boys, who left the churchyard and ran round to the west door. There, though they all knew the church to be empty, they plainly heard the sounds of a man preaching and a congregation singing psalms. By now thoroughly scared, they ran back to the churchyard but were soon playing their games again.

One of the boys who had left his copy-book in the classroom decided, in spite of what he had heard, to go and fetch it. As he entered the empty classroom he suddenly froze, for about six feet away from him, and across one of the benches, lay a heavy coffin. Thoroughly alarmed he rushed back to the churchyard, breathlessly telling the others what he had seen. All twelve of them returned to the classroom and this time they not only all saw the coffin but five of them saw the ghost of John Daniel himself. He sat there in broad daylight, a little apart from the open coffin and looking towards them. The first to recognise the ghost was John Daniel's own half-brother, who at once cried out: 'There sits our John with just such a coat on as I have, with a pen in his hand, a book beside him, and a coffin by him. I'll throw a stone at him.'

The other boys who had by now all pushed into the classroom tried to stop him, but the boy threw the stone and both coffin and ghost vanished before their unbelieving eyes, as they fled in panic from the room. Their story immediately aroused suspicion of foul play in the circumstances of the child's death and the boys were at once summoned to appear before Colonel Broadrep for examination. All of them agreed upon a description of the coffin, some of them even accurately described the hinges. One of the boys, aged twelve, who had never seen Daniel alive and had come to school after that boy's death, said he had not only seen his ghost but had noticed a white cloth or bandage around one of his hands. An exhumation was ordered and a belated inquest held. The last statement was corroborated on oath by the woman who had laid out the corpse and had in fact, removed a white bandage from his hand which he had hurt or cut. Still further damning evidence was given by two women, a joiner, and the chirurgeon. The first two, who had found the body, had seen 'a black list' tied round its neck. The joiner deposed that the shroud was not a normal one but in two parts, one over and one under the body. The chirurgeon would not state positively that the neck had been dislocated but the jury brought in a verdict of 'strangled'.

No further steps were taken to ascertain the murderer even though the people of Beaminster seem to have been satisfied that John Daniel's ghost had returned to the school to prove to his classmates that he had not died a natural death as they believed. If the boy's spirit had wished for revenge it was disappointed, for none was taken, but nevertheless after the true verdict was given by the jury, the ghost never returned again to disturb the children in the schoolyard.

Athelhampton—The six spectres

The splendid fifteenth-century battlemented Athelhampton Hall lies off the main Bournemouth–Dorchester road, five miles north-east of Dorchester and half a mile east of Puddletown. It is one of the finest medieval houses in England, has been used as a family residence for over five centuries, and is open to the public between April and October on three afternoons a week.

Here are indeed riches; splendid panelling, heraldic glass, secret staircases, a timbered Great Hall, a fifteenth-century dovecote, pavilions, gardens with the River Piddle running through them, and for good measure at least six authentically documented ghosts which have been seen by guests and visitors alike very many times. Thomas Hardy called it Athel Hall, and it is supposed to have been the palace of King Athelstan. It has been occupied for many centuries as a family home, and this always adds warmth and atmosphere to a place. So often, if left uninhabited, these large houses become mere rooms, full of beautiful things, but without giving any conviction at all that people could ever really live in them.

The ghosts are the celebrated Grey Lady, (where is she

not?), two duellists, a phantom monkey or ape, a hooded monk dressed in black, and a wine-barrel cooper. Of these, the most famous is the monkey, known as The Spectral Ape, or more familiarly, since it belonged once to the family, the Martyn Ape. Athelhampton was originally built by the first Martyn in the fifteenth century during the Wars of the Roses. The crest of their coat of arms was an ape seated on a tree stump; their motto was: 'He who looks at Martyn's ape, Martyn's ape shall look at him'.

In the Great Chamber, and leading from it to the Long Gallery, is a secret staircase near the fireplace, entered by pressing a secret panel. There, in a small room leading down from the Long Gallery, is the ghost of the Martyn ape. It has been there since the day when one of the Martyn girls, said to have been jilted by her lover, went up the secret stairway to this room, where she killed herself. In her anguish she did not notice that her pet had followed her into the room, the door of which she had shut tightly. The animal, no doubt at first frantic with fear and sorrow at the loss of its mistress, finally starved to death, and its spirit has ever since haunted the room.

It was in the Great Chamber also that a guest one day was quietly reading when, quite unaccountably looking up, she saw the figures of two young men come from nowhere into the vast room and, drawing swords, begin to fight a duel. So realistic were they that she rose and protested, but they took no notice when she cried out to them to stop. By now thoroughly alarmed, she rang the bell for one of the maids to come, but nobody answered her summons. In sheer terror, unable to move, she watched the duelling men as they moved swiftly round the room lunging desperately at each other. When one was slashed across his arm, both of them vanished as silently and swiftly as they had appeared. Later when the guest told her host he refused to believe her story of his extraordinary visitors saying, 'I can't understand what you are talking about; you met all the guests staying here at tea.'

The ghost of the cooper has been both seen and heard in the wine cellar where he is continually beating on non-existent wine barrels with a hammer behind the closed door. The hooded monk in black might well have been the priest who had once been *persona grata* at all times in the house. He wears a black cassock and a shovel hat and wanders about inside and outside the house, without any seeming purpose or direction.

It is in the Tudor Room however, that the ghost of the Grey Lady was seen for the first time, though she has appeared in other parts of the house as well. It was at the end of a day when the house had been open to the public that a housemaid was going through the rooms to make sure that they were empty. When she came to the Tudor Room she saw a lady dressed all in grey sitting in a chair. The housemaid told her that the house was closing and that she was the last visitor, and requested her to leave. The Grey Lady rose and without a word vanished through the wooden panelling at the base of the wall. A housekeeper saw her later still, describing her as 'wearing a plain grey dress and a gauzy sort of head dress'.

There have never been any clues at all to four of the six spectres at Athelhampton Hall. But can there be some link between the Grey Lady and the phantom duellists? Was she perhaps the cause of it all? Were they both her jealous lovers, or one her lover and one her husband? Does she sit and wait in the Tudor Room for the victor to come to her from the Great Chamber to claim her for his own? It is all very intriguing, as all good ghost stories ought to be.

BEAULIEU ABBEY

The chanting monks

Beaulieu Abbey and Palace House, the home of Lord Montagu of Beaulieu, are some fourteen miles south of Southampton and five miles south-east of Lyndhurst in the New Forest. Quite apart from the many attractions which bring over half a million visitors annually, it has many ghosts. They flit about the magnificent ruins and the 11,000 acre estate—kindly, gentle ghosts who are as familiar to the people on the estate and in the village as living people. They chant, hurry about their busy ghost activities, appear at all times, and are most attentive with their masses for the dead. People talk of them, even to them, and they sometimes attend church services.

Yet in spite of their kindliness these ghosts terrified some of the toughest trained people in the world during the last war, when Special Operations Executive took over Beaulieu to train some 100 or more secret agents who were in their final stages of briefing before being dropped by parachute into enemy-held territories. It was a savagely hard training, both physically and mentally, of ceaseless interrogation, warnings of inevitable torture, long periods of privation, and in the use of armed and unarmed combat. Of all these individuals, many of whom never came back, the two most famous agents sent out from Beaulieu were Odette Churchill, who managed to survive prolonged torture, and Violette Szabo, who was executed in the monstrous concentration camp of Ravensbruck. Yet even some of these people, accustomed as they were to danger and to surprises of all sorts, were uneasy in the supernatural atmosphere surrounding Beaulieu at certain times. This atmosphere is caused by monks, notably the one brown monk who has been in permanent occupation, possibly for the 800 years since the great abbey was first built by the White Monks!

The abbot and his thirty monks first came to this beautiful spot which they at once called Beaulieu, after the Anglo-Saxon 'Beo-Lea' in 1204. King John, who had no love for these 'White Monks', as he called them, had threatened to have all their abbots trampled to death, and he drove them out of Berkshire, where they had held the royal manor he himself had given them earlier. Then the king had a dream in which he saw all the assembled monks before a judge who ordered them to scourge their royal persecutor. This they did to such effect that John woke in terror, still feeling the terrible punishment they had dealt out. On the advice of his chaplain and in expiation of his crime, he not only spared the abbots but founded the great abbey of Beaulieu, richly endowed it, and even wished to be buried there.

These 'White Monks' were the Cistercians, who had seceded from the Benedictines in 1089, thus enabling them to fulfil their vows of poverty and obedience, which had seriously lapsed under the Benedictines. Their founder decreed they should build by a stream, far from the conversation of man, and so they began to build the magnificent abbey where the River Exe came down to meet the tidal Beaulieu River at the end of a long creek, and near to the New Forest. So hard did they work to achieve their creation that only forty-two years later, in 1246, the great abbey was completed.

John had died but his son, Henry III, with his queen, children, and several great nobles of the land, came to the dedication of the abbey, and rewarded the abbot by remitting a very heavy fine he had incurred for poaching in the royal New Forest. He was fined again four years later, for the abbot loved game and good hunting. This time he had placed stakes in the abbey close itself, on to which the deer were driven and killed. He had also taken a stag and a buck. The abbey became renowned for its luxury and hospitality, and it held a number of very jealously guarded privileges, such as exemption for the abbot from the expense of attending Parliament; a tun of wine granted annually by Edward III, to be used for mass, which was to be supplied by the most unwilling town of Southampton; and most important of all the right of sanctuary. This meant that any person in the land fleeing from secular justice had the right to seek sanctuary within the abbey, and even to stay there for life, if the abbot was willing. This right was used and accepted during the Wars of the Roses, first by the 'she wolf of France', Margaret of Anjou, wife of the Lancastrian Henry VI, and later by the Countess of Warwick, wife of 'The Kingmaker', on the eve of the battle of Barnet, where he was killed. Although it was a strict rule never to admit women to Cistercian abbeys, the abbot took pity on her and gave her authority to stay. She lived there for fourteen years, until the Wars of the Roses ended and all her lands were restored to her.

But the death knell sounded in 1536 when a covetous and greedy Henry VIII dissolved all the religious houses of England and seized their enormous wealth, though Beaulieu came off better than most. The estate was sold to Thomas Wriothesley, the first earl of Southampton (whose grandson was the renowned patron of Shakespeare) for £1,350 6s 8d, and in 1673 it became the property of the Montagu family. The destruction of the abbey by Henry VIII was brutally thorough, and all that is left today is the superb gatehouse, now the Palace House, one of the most splendid buildings of its kind in England. The great church has gone but there are still some arches standing in the very beautiful cloister;

the refectory and dormitory of the lay brothers, with the stairs that led into the chapel; their dorter, now the museum; the lavatory; the refectory or *frater*, now the parish church; and the *domus conversorum*, now a restaurant, still stand. The acres of surrounding woodlands, pasture, and river, are still the *beau lieu*, the 'beautiful place', the monks first called it nearly 800 years ago.

After the desecration and final demolition of the great abbey so dearly venerated by the monks, it is not at all surprising their ghosts should still flit about searching for what is irretrievably lost, content in their old haunts although so much has been changed and restored. In any case, due to the care and love of the second Baron Montagu, who did so much to restore and beautify the ruins, the monks can still find some communal life on the estate, and there is still a church to worship in.

Until 1939 Beaulieu still guarded its rare privilege of having a private chaplain as well as a parish priest, with no allegiance to a bishop. The last of this special type of incumbent still wore the Cistercian habit and even a mitre, and called himself the Abbot of Beaulieu. It has been said that he not only deeply believed in the presence of the ghost monks but even spoke to them, so that the villagers quite jokingly inquired of him how such and such a lay brother was. This abbot even held special and closed services for the ghost monks, usually on Christmas Eve, so why should they ever want to leave Beaulieu? Once, in answer to a villager's statement that 'the church was not very well attended today' the abbot answered: 'On the contrary, it was full!'—thinking of the many ghost monks who were there.

But it is the brown monk who is most frequently seen, and he it was who frightened some of those tough secret agents. This was not from any spirit of evil or unkindness on his part, for the many witnesses who have seen him have found him to be kind, gentle, and unobtrusive. He has been seen in the cloisters, once holding a parchment or scroll; beyond the medieval wine-press; once wearing a long habit almost like a skirt; and many other times, gently moving about his ghostly business.

The most remarkable ghost features of Beaulieu, or indeed of anywhere else in England, is the wonderful chanting which has been heard many times at night across the lawns. It is obviously some kind of requiem mass, since it invariably follows or immediately precedes the death of a person in the village or the vicinity, and is only ever heard at night. Sometimes it is very loud and then dies away and returns; it has been described by those who have heard it as a very beautiful form of Gregorian plainsong, and was actually notated on a piano by one listener and immediately recognised by someone else as the chanting he had himself previously heard. Once, curiously linked to this singing, the sounds of footsteps and digging were heard in a garden, as if preparations were being made for a burial, and indeed both actually happened on the eve of a villager's death. There has also been a strong smell of incense at various times.

All this is in complete harmony with the continuation of the medieval monastic life of prayer, offices, discipline, obedience and peace. On the north-east side of the church was the former burial-ground of the monks, but no skeletons have ever been found, probably because coffins were never used by the brethren, only shrouds which could easily have caused complete disintegration of the buried dead during the succeeding centuries. Ghosts have also been seen and heard here, as if they were busy with a burial service, and this has struck more fear in people than all their other actions put together. Another reason for the presence of the ghostly monks may be connected with an inscription set up in the beautiful garden of peace by the second Baron Montagu in gratitude to God for his miraculous escape in World War I, when his ship was torpedoed and he was in the water for eighteen hours; also in memory of his secretary who lost her life there. This was a long and anxious time for his family, who had no idea if he were alive or dead, until one day the private chaplain, he who proudly called himself the 'Abbot of Beaulieu' brought them good news from the 'other world'. He said that he had seen Lord Montagu quite clearly walking in front of him down the village street. Then in a strange sentence he added, 'If he were dead he would have been walking behind me.' Almost immediately afterwards news came of his rescue.

When the second baron eventually died in 1929, a tablet put up by his son simply reads: 'He loved Beaulieu, deeming his possession of it a sacred trust to be handed on to his successors in like manner.'

Can this beautiful chanting, which brings peace and harmony and joy to all who hear it, be a requiem mass constantly sung for the man who did so much to make the abbey what it is today? These splendid ruins belong to the monks, so too the beautiful cloister, the troughs they hollowed out from tree trunks felled in the New Forest and used as water-pipes, and the exquisite pulpit in the present church, built as a rostrum from which the monks once read at meal times to their silent brethren below. If all this were not enough to keep them at Beaulieu, still outlined on the grass are the nave, aisle, chapels and transepts of the once splendid thirteenth-century abbey which was built by their own hands. Is it then so strange that these monks should continue to stay in so well-loved a place when they are so obviously happy in their centuries-old home.

HINTON AMPNER MANOR

The skull in the box

Of all the many haunted houses in England, there are very few whose sense of evil, mystery and fear has been so terrifying that the house has not only driven out all its occupants, but has finally had to be demolished. One of these places was the manor of Hinton Ampner in Hampshire, nine miles east of Winchester and four from Alresford, above the lovely Meon valley. The record of all the events which took place there is probably the most carefully and certainly the most accurately documented history of ghosts or poltergeists designedly left by the writer to posterity. The wonder is not so much that the mother deliberately wrote all this down for her children to read later, but that she was able, physically and mentally, to continue living there as long as she did. Indeed she was finally compelled to leave only upon her brother's absolute insistence that she should do so.

The original manor house was built in the early seventeenth century, probably 1623, by Sir Thomas Stewkley, and continued to be occupied by his descendants for almost a century. On 10 May 1719, Mary Stewkley married Edward Stawell. He was heir to the barony of that name and ten years younger than his wife. They set up house together in Hinton Ampner and Mary's younger sister, Honoria, continued to live there as before. For twenty years they all enjoyed the normal and uneventful life of a large comfortable country house, with plenty of servants, the usual life led by most of the eighteenth-century richer class.

Mary died in July 1740, and Honoria continued to care for

her brother-in-law as best she could, for he did not wish to alter his way of life. Two years later he succeeded to the title of Baron Stawell. It was not long before whispers and rumours began to filter down, from the servants in the big house to the village and beyond, that the master and his sister-in-law seemed to be much closer to each other than was usual or desirable in such a relationship. In fact there was a liaison between them. The next piece of gossip eagerly taken up by the villagers was that a child had been secretly born up at the house. No sooner was this piece of information digested than another, even grimmer titbit announced the mysterious disappearance of the child; 'might even have been done away with' as it was crudely put. This was just the beginning of a long chain of mysterious events.

Honoria died in November 1754, at the age of sixty-six, and a plaque to her memory was put up by Lord Stawell in the village church. On 2 April 1755, Lord Stawell was quietly sitting in the parlour of the manor house when he had an apoplectic stroke. He managed to utter one inarticulate sentence before passing into a coma, and died the next morning. He was fifty-six and left a daughter, his only son having predeceased him while still at Westminster School.

Not long after Lord Stawell died, his bailiff and house steward, Isaac Machrel, as sinister a character as his master was said to be, came to a sudden end, apparently caused by the fall of a heavy pile of firewood. Gossip also implied that the bailiff had had some strange hold over his master, for, though he had been caught red-handed in some act of dishonesty, he had been kept on in the baron's service. This, however, has never been corroborated, but was a high point in the drama of Hinton Ampner Manor.

A few days later, Lord Stawell's groom was in his bedroom one bright moonlit night, when he clearly saw the ghost of his master in the drab coat he always used to wear. The manor had remained unoccupied for some time though a number of the servants had been retained to look after the place for the shooting season. In January 1765, Hinton Ampner Manor was let to a certain Mr Ricketts, a wealthy West Indian landowner whose business frequently took him to Jamaica, but who wished to rent a house where his wife and family could live during his absences. He could never have foreseen how unfortunate his choice would become; it is quite obvious that no rumours or gossip of what had taken place reached his ears, or he would never have entered into the tenancy agreement. He brought his own domestic staff, who had no knowledge of what had occurred, a very important factor in the light of future events. Mrs Ricketts herself came from the distinguished and wealthy family of Jervis, her brother being later created Earl St Vincent in recognition of his gallant naval achievements. She was known for her absolute truthfulness, a most significant fact in view of her subsequent meticulous and accurate account of all the events which took place. She called this document 'Mary Ricketts' legacy to her children'.

Exactly a century later this was published in *The Gentleman's Magazine* as 'A Hampshire Ghost Story', one of the most astonishing and frightening records anyone has ever made in the history of the occult. The Ricketts family had no sooner settled in their new home than the first strange disturbances began. Doors were heavily slammed shut, though none had been left open, and, in spite of having new locks put on them throughout the house, they still continued to slam. In the summer of that year Mrs Ricketts writes:

> Elizabeth Brelsford, nurse to our eldest son Henry, aged eight months, was sitting by him when asleep in a room over the pantry appropriated for the nursery, and being a hot summer's evening the door was open that faces the entrance into the Yellow Bed-chamber, which with the adjoining dressing room was the apartment usually occupied by the lady of the house. She was sitting

directly opposite to this door and plainly saw, as she afterwards related, a gentleman in a drab coloured suit of clothes go into the Yellow Room.

The nurse thought nothing of this, and when the maid-servant brought up her supper she asked her who was the gentleman who had gone into the Yellow Room? The servant had seen no one, but they both began a search, finding no trace of anybody. Elizabeth was by then quite disturbed, for in the clear light of that summer evening she knew she had quite distinctly seen a figure in a drab coat. What she did not know was that it was almost exactly ten years since Lord Stawell's groom had seen the very same figure and recognised it as his master.

Mrs Ricketts herself thought nothing more about the incident until that autumn when one of the grooms, crossing the Great Hall to go to bed, saw at the other end a figure in a drab-coloured coat. He thought this was the new butler, who wore such clothes because his livery had not yet been made for him, but when he entered the room where the male staff slept he saw the butler fast asleep on his bed. Accounts of the same apparition given by two different people increased Mrs Ricketts' growing fears—though she kept them to herself—that all was not right in the house.

A year later, towards the end of a July evening, a number of servants, having a meal together in the kitchen, heard a woman come downstairs and along the passage leading towards them, her clothes rustling as if they were made of stiff silk. The door was open and they clearly saw the figure of a woman rush past and out of the house, and described her as 'a tall figure in dark-coloured clothes'. Another servant, who came in from outside at the same time was asked who the woman was, and answered, to their united astonishment, that he had seen no one at all.

The noises, now much louder, began again—slamming

doors, footsteps, rustlings round the beds, and deep, long groans, as of someone in great pain or grief. Some of the servants obviously did not want to stay in a house which they now knew was haunted and left. Mrs Ricketts herself was disturbed, one night, in bed in the Yellow Room, by the sound of a man's heavy footsteps drawing nearer and nearer to her locked door. So alarmed was she that she sprang out of bed, but at this, the sounds ceased. She then began changing her room, always having them prepared quite late at night in order to avoid any possibility of her plans reaching this evil spirit if this was what it was. She had, one night, changed again from the Yellow Room to the Chintz Room above the entrance porch, where she heard not only music but three distinct and violent knocks, as if a club had been used on the door of a room below.

In the year 1771 a new sound came to the house; this was a strange hollow murmuring, and on 2 April Mrs Ricketts heard the footsteps, not of one but of two people, in the adjoining lobby, and of someone trying to push open the door, for a period of over twenty terrifying minutes. So real was this experience that she rang her bell for one of the menservants to come, but, in spite of careful searching, there was nothing unusual in any of the rooms. It now seemed clear that wherever Mrs Ricketts decided to sleep she was disturbed, either by three loud knocks, groans, murmurings as of a very high wind, footsteps, shuffling or rustling. In one single night she changed her room no less than three times and in the last, over the entrance, she heard the front door slam with such violence that it shook the whole room. It was only then, for the first time since her husband had gone away, that she decided to have one of her servants always sleeping in the room with her. 'I then became convinced', she wrote, 'that what was taking place was beyond the power of any mortal agent to perform.'

After midsummer the noises became more and more intolerable and continuous, often at intervals all through the night, preventing sleep, causing irritability and tiredness by day and a dread of going to bed at night. She began to hear a shrill female voice interspersed with men's deeper voices, as if arguing or joining in a conversation, though the words were indistinguishable. Then there were other more harmonious sounds, walking, more talking, doors opening and slamming, the drawing aside of bedcurtains, not once but every single night, and every one of these sounds was confirmed by the maid sleeping in the room with her. It is quite beyond belief that the members of the household could have continued to live in this now evil house, or that they managed to avoid serious nervous breakdowns.

When her brother came home from the Mediterranean to stay with her, quite inexplicably she said nothing to him. After his departure however, when she and her maid had gone to sleep in the same room:

> I heard with infinite astonishment the most loud, deep, tremendous noise which seemed to rush and fall with infinite velocity and force on the whole lobby floor adjoining to my room. I started up and called to my maid 'Good God! did you hear that noise?' It was some time before the maid could answer, and then only in a faltering, choking voice, saying she was too frightened to speak. Just at that instant we heard a shrill and dreadful shriek that seemed to proceed from under the spot where the rushing noise fell, repeated three or four times and growing fainter as it seemed to descend till it sank into the earth.

The nurse, sleeping in the same room with the children, was so appalled that for two hours she was totally deprived of speech. 'This alarm, so more than commonly horrible, determined me to impart the whole thing to my brother.' It was not too soon, for already Mary Ricketts' health was deteriorating alarmingly, as she herself relates, breaking out into a kind of fever from continued lack of sleep and sustained fear. Her brother's naval duties compelled him to remain a further week at Portsmouth, during which time all the same frightening noises continued with greater frequency and strength than ever.

At last Mrs Ricketts was able to tell her brother the whole story. With his neighbour and friend, Captain Luttrell, he arranged to keep a close watch that night to get to the bottom of the mystery, revealing nothing to any of the servants. The whole house was thoroughly searched from top to bottom, the doors shut and bolted in the unused rooms and all locks and window clasps tested before the two men, both armed, settled for the night. Mrs Ricketts' brother left strict instructions to be called at the slightest alarm. He sat in the Yellow Room, his manservant and Captain Luttrell shared the Chintz Room, and Mrs Ricketts slept in another room on the same floor, so that all the rooms were occupied. Mrs Ricketts had no sooner got into bed than she heard the rustle of a stiff silk dress quite near her; almost immediately the door of the Chintz Room was flung open violently and Captain Luttrell cried out loudly: 'Who goes there?' He heard footsteps coming from the lobby and felt something rush past him. The noise continued until it reached the brother's door. He was by now fully awake and the three men began an immediate search of the whole house, but everything was as they had left it before going to bed.

The men returned to sit up until dawn, when Mrs Ricketts' brother went to his own room. She writes: 'About that time I imagine I heard the Chintz Room door opened and slammed to with the utmost violence and immediately that of the hall chamber opened and shut in the same manner. An hour later I heard the house door open and shut in the same way so as to shake the house.'

At breakfast that morning the two men had already decided that Mrs Ricketts must no longer live in the house and that arrangements must be made to move; to arrange this her brother decided to stay another week. The sounds continued, and there was one terrifying moment when Mrs Ricketts heard the sound of a pistol being fired, followed by terrible groans as though of a dying person—no one else heard this. The brother tried to sleep in the daytime. One afternoon he rang his bell for help for he felt as though some immense weight had dropped from the ceiling on to his body. Throughout these last days both Mrs Ricketts' cat and spaniel behaved in the strangest possible manner, slinking under chairs and refusing to come out again.

About August 1771, some seven years after the Ricketts family moved in, Mrs Ricketts accepted the offer of accommodation at the Old Palace by the Bishop of Winchester. What finally drove her from Hinton Ampner was a single isolated incident. 'I was assailed by a noise I never heard before, very near me, and the terror I felt is not to be described.'

Rewards were offered by Lady Hillsborough, Lord Stawell's daughter, rising from £50 to £100 for any clue to whatever it was that haunted the manor house, but no reward was ever claimed. Almost a year later the manor was let to a Mr Lawrence and his family. They had scarcely settled in when the apparition of a woman was seen, and they fled in terror from the house and never returned. It remained empty until 1797 when it was finally demolished; later a new house was built some fifty yards away.

During the demolition the workmen found under the floor of a lobby near the Yellow Room a small box, which contained a small skull, thought to be that of a monkey but also claimed to belong to a baby or very young child. In this long chain of events which took place in Hinton Ampner Manor during those seven years, surely nothing was stranger than the discovery of the skull. Was it that of the child said to be born to Honoria by her brother-in-law, Lord Stawell? Were they the unhappy, terrifying ghosts who finally drove the Ricketts family and then the Lawrences out?

Some years later a dying woman, once employed by Lord Stawell, expressed a wish to speak to a member of the Jervis family, but died before she could do so. It was said that Lord St Vincent would never discuss the subject with anyone and that he either knew full well, or could guess, what she had to say. History is silent on these things and no one will ever know.

A COTSWOLDS TRIO

Burford—The Priory Ghosts

The Oxfordshire town of Burford is unquestionably one of the most beautiful in the Cotswolds, and is greatly loved by residents and tourists. It is only a pity that its popularity is causing it to become commercialised, like so many other English towns. Its impressive church, Tudor houses, Georgian façades, ancient and splendid inns, almshouses and its charming bridge across the River Windrush attract thousands of visitors throughout the year. Americans especially, love this beautiful corner of England, for its green and generous countryside, its honey-coloured stone cottages with their distinctive roofs, and its ancient churches. As far back as the seventh century it was considered to be one of the most important towns in Wessex and worth defending at all costs. The town's armies raided and defeated Ethelbald, King of Mercia, in AD 753, and this victory established the town's supremacy right through the centuries and down to the present day. It has become progressively prosperous through its stone work, cloth weaving, and paper manufacture.

Burford Priory, haunted since its foundation in the early thirteenth century, has never been regarded by any of its numerous owners as a happy place. Poltergeists have been at work, throwing things about, doors have been opened and closed, unexplained footsteps, knocks on doors and walls, and ringing bells and screams have been heard. Not a place, you would imagine, to encourage inhabitants, yet it has rarely been empty, nor has anyone actually been driven out. Today it is occupied by a closed order and in spite of ceaseless prayers from the peaceful nuns living there, the ghosts have never been fully exorcised. Curiously enough their presence never alarms, only mystifies, and in a strange way pleases, through long familiarity with their ways and appearances.

The most familiar ghost is a gardener, dressed like an old gamekeeper, carrying an old-fashioned gun in the crook of his arm. In 1695 Lord Abercorn was tried for murdering a man named John Prior in the summer house of the monks' burial ground in the priory, but was acquitted, 'a gardener being hanged instead', as history callously records. This ghost is almost certainly that of this unfortunate and hideously wronged man.

The entrance hall of the priory, with its huge Tudor fireplace and stone flagging, is haunted by a second ghost, a small monk dressed and cowled in brown, who has been seen by many different people at various times of the day and night. Once one of the nuns actually cried out to the priory gardener mowing the lawn, warning him of the monk before its ghost disappeared, but the gardener did not see it. This spirit has been seen in almost every corner of the building together with the sound of monks singing their offices. Many times nuns in chapel have distinctly heard footsteps in the passage leading to the robing room, believing them to be those of the chaplain, who, however, was nowhere to be seen. At two o'clock in the morning a mysterious bell peals loudly, calling the nuns to an office which took place in medieval times and has since ceased. A robed and cowled figure in black has often been seen by nuns aroused by the bell, and some, new and unfamiliar with the priory, have arisen from their beds at the urgent summons of the bell, even dressing and hurrying to chapel.

The old rectory, linked with the priory by a cobbled path, is disturbed at night by heavy footsteps, and once, quite recently, by terrifying screams heard in an attic. This was particularly alarming, for it is believed that hundreds of years ago a man was murdered in one of these upper attics.

Burford Priory is a fine old house, probably founded by the Earl of Gloucester in the twelfth century as a hospital of St John the Evangelist. It is not officially mentioned, however, until 1226, when it received a royal grant of firewood from the nearby Wychwood Forest. A master and three brethren lived there until the reign of Henry VIII, tending the sick and needy and giving hospitality to poor and weary travellers. When the priory was dissolved with all the other monasteries and religious houses, Henry gave it to his barber-surgeon, Edmund Harman, but he never lived there and let it go to rack and ruin.

The priory next came into the hands of Sir Laurence Tanfield, who built a splendid Elizabethan mansion on its ruins. It was during his ownership that the great days of the priory began, but he died unmourned by the people of Burford. The priory was inherited by his grandson, Lucius Cary, Viscount Falkland, the celebrated Cavalier, but so heavily encumbered by debts that he was forced to sell it in 1637, for the sum of £7,000, to one of his trustees, William Lenthall, the renowned Speaker of the Long Parliament. It was he who rebuked Charles I when he entered the House of Commons demanding to know the whereabouts of the five members who had only just escaped. Lenthall's reply is immortal: 'I have, Sir, neither eyes to see nor tongue to speak in this place but as the House is pleased to direct me, whose servant I am.'

Lenthall greatly improved and still further beautified his mansion, and, an art lover, filled it with valuable pictures from Charles I's splendid collection after the king's execution. William Lenthall's son John inherited the priory, 'the grand Bragadaccio and Lyar of the age he lived in' as Anthony Wood viciously summed him up, and it was he who received

Charles II there, as well as Nell Gwynne, whose room is still named after her. When Nell's bastard son by the king was created Duke of St Albans, Charles also conferred on him the title of Earl of Burford, to commemorate his visit to that town.

The priory was later bought by Sir Archibald Southby MP. In 1947 he handed it over to the Benedictine Order of the Salutation of the Blessed Virgin Mary, for he and his wife were convinced that it would never be a happy place until it was returned to the church. During their ownership they experienced calamity after calamity and one of the worst of these befell Sir Archibald when, with a delegation from Parliament, he made a visit of inspection to the dreaded Nazi concentration camp of Buchenwald. There he fell ill and declined to such an extent that he was forced to retire from his parliamentary life.

The priory's history is a troubled one. It suffered from the deep division of the Civil War and one, possibly even two murders inside and outside the house, have done nothing to improve the unhappiness and restlessness of the place. The peace and calm it has gained from the sisters of the closed order have done much to allay and quieten these disorders, but the priory is not yet completely free of its ghosts, and perhaps never will be.

Swinbrook—The haunted vicarage

Some two miles east of Burford along the enchanting valley of the Windrush is the charming little Cotswold village of Swinbrook. Here, for 300 years, in the splendid manor house they built, lived the ubiquitous Fettiplace family, who did nothing at all of note throughout these six centuries except amass wealth and marry into still richer families. Nothing is left today of the splendid manor house which Anthony

Fettiplace built in 1503, and which, according to contemporary writers, was one of the finest in England. Its vast banqueting hall proudly displayed their many coats-of-arms in stained-glass windows under the great oak roof. They built fine stables, great rose terraces and fish-ponds, and their servants wore the green livery of the Fettiplaces. Today all has gone. Walking across the fields which were once part of their vast estate one can see the faint outlines of the rose terraces and the fish-ponds, but no trace whatsoever of one single stone of the former house.

Neither in war nor in peace did they distinguish themselves to any great degree, concentrating on becoming great landowners, owning no less than forty-seven manors and thousands of acres of land and woodland. They did however, found many charities, a number of them rich even today, and these they left to posterity—together with an exceedingly beautiful church, one of the loveliest in the Cotswolds. Here, in the chancel, six life-size effigies lie under their coats-of-arms. All of them are in armour, three resting their heads on their hands as if dozing or reflecting on what they believed they had achieved, with self-satisfied and slightly arrogant features. Three of them lean forward, resting on their elbows as if preparing for something, alert, their eyes expectant, perhaps visualising another land deal.

Their ghosts haunt not only the chancel—an armed and kneeling figure once very clearly seen by a friend of the late vicar—but the vicarage too. In recent years all their ghosts have been seen or heard many times. When the late vicar and his wife first went to live in the vicarage, they heard almost at once strange, indefinable sounds which they thought were due to the expansion and contraction of walls in winter and summer. These sounds however, soon gave evidence of something much more significant. Many times footsteps were heard running up the stairs, followed by the opening and closing of the bedroom door above the sitting-room which they normally used. In this room a small wooden cradle frequently began rocking without any visible signs as to who was moving it, although the rocking always seemed to be accompanied by the sound of a deep sigh.

Sometimes the footsteps up and down the stairs were so clear and loud that their dog would stand barking at the walls, his hair on end, teeth bared, puzzled and angry. Sometimes the dog would start growling, looking towards the window. His mistress, believing he had heard cats, would encourage him to go after them, but he would not go near the window, instead crouching down and growling. Sometimes, too, the dog would rise from sleep on the rug before the fire and stand growling threateningly at an armchair where a ghost-like figure quite obviously sat, which only the dog could sense, but nothing would induce him to go near the chair.

Upstairs, on the bedroom floor, a ghost has been seen standing at the end of the corridor by the late vicar's daughter. One of the bedrooms is recognised as a haunted room. The vicar's wife always provided candles, matches and night-lights for her guests staying in it, telling them to call out if they were disturbed. The writer remembers feeling strangely uneasy when he slept there, and did in fact keep a night-light burning, though he was never visited by a ghost.

In their own bedroom a singular event took place when one night the vicar's wife woke up, calling out that she was very hot, and sat bolt upright in bed to get cool. When she lay down again she felt an icy coldness beside her and knew that the ghost was in her bed. Though afraid to move she knew it would go just as the others always did, for they were now familiar figures in the house and never seemed to do any harm at all.

There was also speculation about an armed and kneeling figure at the altar rails. Could this perhaps be Sir John Fettiplace, 'who died verie suddenly, not without suspition of his being poyson'd by his wife Susanna'? After his death his wife was summoned before the justices but as nothing could be proved against her the case was dismissed and she went to live at Lechlade, 'and took to her there a husband, a brisk, gay, and handsome young man, Sir Thomas Cutler, for of Sir John she was weary, he being a dul fellow.' So perhaps it was he who came to pray, not only for her soul, but for better luck in her new venture. This kneeling figure could even be that of Sir George, last of the male line, whose splendid bust is on the right side of the chancel, his pleasant, humorous face gazing across at his six ancestors. Sir George had several mistresses during his hectic lifetime and did all he could to beget an heir, but failed. He loved horse-racing, cock-fighting, gambling, drinking and women. He died from a stroke, after a violent quarrel in the Bull Inn, Burford, where he was always to be found—his death as dramatic as his life had been. As one cannot really imagine Sir George at the altar rails, it is more likely that he is the cause of the disturbances in the vicarage which so bothered the dog.

This kneeling figure might not even be a Fettiplace at all but a certain Mr Freeman. After the sudden death of Sir George, the great manor house of Swinbrook had this gentleman as a tenant which produced a very curious epilogue to the whole Fettiplace history, and not one they would have relished. Mr Freeman arrived, and lived there in high style, liked by villagers and gentry alike, entertaining lavishly and keeping open house for all and sundry.

At that time mail-coaches and lone riders on the highways were becoming more and more frequently attacked and robbed, especially on the nearby London–Gloucester road. Complaints came in from everywhere and the people in Swinbrook and Burford were afraid to travel at all. Matters came to a head when a coach was attacked, and in the ensuing skirmish one of the highwaymen was shot, wounded, and arrested. This was none other than Mr Freeman of Swinbrook Manor. It turned out that he had a long record of crime as a highwayman, enough to be condemned to death by hanging in the customary fashion.

After this the manor house fell into decay and decline until nothing of it remained. Yet on second thoughts the ghost could not be Mr Freeman, for by the time of coaches and highwaymen, armour had long since ceased to be worn and the kneeling figure is clearly described as armed. So the speculation must continue and this ghost and others go on haunting both church and vicarage.

Minster Lovell—The haunted ruins

The splendid ruin of the great Lovel mansion is about midway between Burford and Witney, and not only the ruin but even the road leading to it, is haunted. It is said that a huge black cloud sometimes appears low in the sky, driving animals frantic and giving car-drivers a terrifying and totally inexplicable feeling.

The mansion itself was superbly situated and designed, and was built in 1430 by the seventh Baron Lovel. It is backed by a great line of trees of the former royal forest of Wychwood, and ran right down to the beautiful River Windrush, in whose waters the ruins are impressively reflected. Even today the magnificent ruins of a fifty-foot-high west tower, banqueting hall, great windows and vaulted passages are a fine example of domestic architecture of that period, while the dovecote must be one of the finest in England. The seventh baron also built the beautiful fifteenth-century church in which his effigy lies in plate armour on a splendid alabaster tomb covered with the coats-of-arms of his own and allied families. The mansion was built on the site of a small, ancient priory attached to the Abbey of Ivry in Normandy, so Minster was added to the name of Lovell. It is now in the care of the Department of the Environment, who make a nominal charge for entry. In autumn, when the mist comes down over the gaunt ruins, and the winding river gathers the falling leaves from the colourful trees dripping with rain, it is not difficult to feel the whole place is haunted, as indeed it is, not singly but doubly.

The legend of the Mistletoe Bough is also claimed by Bramshill, now a police college, and Marwell Hall, both in Hampshire. The Minster Lovell version is that one Christmas Eve, when a great party was being held, a game of hide-and-seek was organised and Lovel's young bride ran away and hid herself. She was never seen again, in spite of desperate and anxious searches everywhere. It was not until many years later that her skeleton was found, hidden in an oak chest into which she had climbed and been trapped when the heavy lid came down on her head. Her restless and unhappy ghost flits through the ruins as she tries to find her young husband once more.

The Bramshill version is similar except that the girl ran away playfully from her young lover during a dance, but her end and the manner of her death were the same. In this case verses about the legend have been preserved.

> The mistletoe hung in the castle hall
> The holly bough hung on the old oak wall,
> And the Baron's retainers were blithe and gay
> And keeping their Christmas holiday.
> The Baron beheld with a father's pride
> His beautiful child, young Lovel's bride,
> While she with her bright eyes seemed to be
> The star of that elderly company.
> 'I weary of dancing now', she cried,

'Here tarry a moment I'll hide, I'll hide.
And Lovel be sure thou art first to trace
The clue to my secret hiding place.'
So off she ran and her friends began
Each tower to search but each looked askan,
And Lovel cried 'Oh where dost thou hide?
I'm lonesome without thee my own dear bride.'
They sought her that night and they sought her
    next day,
They sought her in vain while a week passed away,
In the highest, the lowest, the loneliest spot,
Young Lovel sought wildly but found her not.
And the years flew by till their grief at last
Was told as a sorrowful tale long past.
And when Lovel appeared the children cried
'See the old man weeps for his fairy bride.'
At length an oak chest which long lay hid
Was found in the castle; they raised the lid
A skeleton form lay mouldering there
In the bridal wreath of that lady fair.
Oh sad was her fate, in sportive jest
She hid from her lord in the old oak chest;
It closed with a spring and dreadful doom
The bride lay clasped in her living tomb.

A curiously similar fate befell another Lovel, Francis the ninth baron, who attained some of the highest honours in the land during Richard III's reign. Such was his power that he was lampooned all over the country in the now familiar rhyme:

> The catte, the ratte and Lovel our dogge
> Rulyth all England under a hogge

The cat was Sir William Catesby, the rat Sir Richard Ratcliffe, Lovel the dog (from his crest) and the hog was the king himself. Lovel fought with the king at Bosworth, whence he escaped to Flanders, while his sovereign was killed. Backed by Margaret, Duchess of Burgundy, Richard III's widowed sister, he arrived in England again at the head of 2,000 Yorkist troops to support Lambert Simnel, pretender to the throne by his claim to be the Earl of Warwick, son of the late king's elder brother Clarence, and therefore lawful king of England. They met Henry VII's troops at Stoke and were routed; once more the luckless Lovel escaped, but this time he disappeared forever. He was last seen swimming the river, and, failing to climb the opposite bank, was believed to have been carried away by the current and drowned.

In the reign of Henry VIII it became necessary to establish his death by some evidence because of the legal disposal of his property and the continuance of his title. A jury ruled that he had escaped beyond the sea and died abroad, and this verdict, though totally unsubstantiated, was accepted by the king. Even before that time rumours had come to Minster Lovell that he was not dead but had returned disguised and secretly hidden himself somewhere, perhaps even in his own mansion, though no one had ever seen him. The mystery of his death had never been explained, but it was reasonably assumed, and finally accepted by all who knew him, that he was alive somewhere, and that one of his trusted servants was looking after him. As the centuries passed it became as much a legend as the Mistletoe Bough, and it was not until the year 1708 that part of the tragic mystery was solved.

Four people, one a monk, determined to solve the mystery themselves, and during excavating operations they discovered, hidden behind an old chimney, a secret chamber. They all saw the skeleton of a man sitting at a table, with a book, paper, and pens upon it. In a corner lay a mouldering cap of the Tudor period. Then before their horrified eyes the skeleton crumbled to dust on its contact with the air. There seemed little doubt it was Lord Lovel, who had found his way home and into this secret room, probably giving strict orders to his servant not to disclose his hiding place. But either the servant died, or lost the key, or merely let his master starve to death and then robbed him of the treasure he knew was also hidden in the house. It will never be fully explained, but his ghost constantly haunts the place. And so in the gaunt ruins of a once magnificent house these two restless spirits glide about their former home. They have been seen many times, often when the moon floods down over this gem of medieval architecture.

Another ghost inhabits the White Hart public house in the High Street. 'Rosalind', as she has been called for some unknown reason, has caused minor troubles on many occasions, throwing glasses from shelves on to the floor and once, by way of variation, and perhaps because she is musical, thowing a handbell to join the broken sherry glasses, all in true poltergeist fashion. She wears a veil, is weeping bitterly whenever she is seen, and that always in the brewery room near a spiral staircase to the loft. On that staircase she hanged herself because of unrequited love. But whoever it was that gave her the name of Rosalind has never been known.

In all England there can surely be no smaller area with so many ghosts than this beautiful corner of the Cotswolds.

RYCOTE HOUSE AND CHAPEL

The mysterious Arabella

'Rycote Chapel Ancient Monument', said the sign, pointing in the direction of a long drive sweeping away through a great park where cattle grazed peacefully in the heat of that English summer afternoon. We had come from the fine town of Thame, some three miles away, where John Hampden had gone to die from the mortal wound he received at Chalgrove Field during the Civil War, and where, in the splendid cruciform parish church, we had seen the superb white marble table tomb of Lord Williams of Thame. It seemed right, therefore, to see what remained of the stately Tudor house where he had once lived.

I could still see that tomb, upon which lay his recumbent effigy and that of his first wife Elizabeth. The carving of his face was accurate, showing his high, polished, domed forehead, his crafty mouth and stern features, not unlike those of Edward VII. He wore his splendid suit of mail which, it is said, he left in his will to the Duke of Bedford. In contrast were the serene, calm, beautiful features of his wife, in her exquisite Tudor costume. But I remembered the tomb more because their effigies lay with their heads to the east, something rarely seen in monumental tombs. In 1841 the tomb was found to be empty, and it has been said that it was desecrated and rifled during the Civil War, when Cromwellian troops had the lead coffin melted down to provide bullets for their guns.

Now we walked the few yards from the car park and there, almost hidden by the trees, we could see the crow-step gables, the fine chimneys, and the stables, all that remained of what was once one of the most splendid Tudor mansions in England, greatly enlarged and beautified in 1539 by Lord Williams of Thame, at present converted into attractive private residences. To the right of the house stood Rycote Chapel, built almost a century earlier, in 1449, by Richard Quartermain and his wife Sibill, as perfect a gem of Perpendicular interior architecture as anywhere in England, with its splendid Renaissance canopied pews. It is shaded from the summer heat by an immense yew, a mighty tree, still flourishing, planted for the coronation of King Stephen in 1135 by the Benedictine monks who had a cell here.

On that lovely summer day, sitting under the tree in this peaceful corner of Oxfordshire, where time suddenly seemed to stand still, it was impossible, even perhaps discordant, to remember the ghosts there, no less than four, but kindly, unobtrusive, quietly going about their several duties. The Earl of Leicester, supposed murderer of his wife Amy Robsart; Sir Thomas More; the brown monk; and gentlest of all, and the most mysterious, the Tudor grey lady affectionately known to all there as Arabella. The genial and kind custodian, Mr Morris, who has seen her once and waits eagerly to do so again, has minutely described her in his little book *Rycote Reflections*, but it is when he talks to you, as he gladly does of her, that she springs to life.

He first saw her one grey winter afternoon in December when the moon was coming up and he was about to lock up and go home. Without any fear at all he began to follow her; as he himself says in his *Rycote Reflections*:

Now she has been, her form quite visible:
one Sunday afternoon, near to Full Moon,
a grey December, the grey figure came:

she walked around the Chapel, as 'twas said
she did: a friendly spirit, so she seemed,
gliding, she lingered not: she just passed by
the eastern end, and all along the north,
to double doors; then turned and went away
towards the site of Williams's Great House,
and vanished out of sight, so suddenly.
Her figure was indeed of grey, and clear,
with sheen of light enveloping the whole,
and in the Tudor style: a ground-length dress,
square neck, tight waist, and with large heavy sleeves:
close fitting head-dress, with a flowing veil:
jewel decoration and embroidery
were both profuse: all this was plain to see—
the outline was distinct, and very clear.

But who Arabella was has remained a close secret, although her Tudor dress gives one slender clue, as may be seen later.

After the death of the Quartermains the Rycote estate passed into the hands of Sir Richard Fowler, himself a reckless spendthrift whose two successive wives were as bad, so that he was finally forced to sell Rycote, which he did in 1521 during a visit to London. The purchaser was John Heron, whose son Giles married Cicely, youngest daughter of Sir Thomas More. Both these men were beheaded by Henry VIII for alleged high treason. It is not therefore surprising to know that the ghost of Sir Thomas More has more than once been seen in the chapel, and by one visitor who did not even know he had ever stayed there. There can be no doubt that on his many visits to Rycote, which he loved as much as did his daughter and son-in-law, he always went to service in the chapel; indeed, he may well have preached there. One of the visitors who saw his ghost spoke of it with perfect calm and serenity as if he had just seen a living person, even a familiar figure, not in any way perturbed or uneasy, so that Sir Thomas More's ghost can only be a peaceful one, contented to be in such a beautiful chapel as Rycote.

After the executions of both her husband and her father no more is heard of Cicely. So why should she not be Arabella herself? It may easily be her ghost searching for her loved ones, for the house her husband did so much to beautify and which is now no more. There is no doubt at all about one thing and that is the costume Arabella wears is of the same period as Cicely's.

The manor and house next came into the hands of Lord Williams of Thame, and there he and his first wife were host and hostess to Henry VIII and his fifth wife Catherine Howard when they came over from Ewelme to spend the rest of their honeymoon at Rycote. In a few months Catherine too would be beheaded. Sir John Williams was wealthy and held the highest offices, including Master of the Royal Jewels. He pursued his own interests with intelligence, subtlety, and cunning, and was not too scrupulous about church matters, since he served four successive sovereigns with diametrically opposed religious beliefs. He profited enormously from the Dissolution of the Monasteries, being at the time Visitor to the Monasteries under the evil Thomas Cromwell.

When Queen Mary married Philip of Spain, Lord Williams was made Lord Chamberlain and was present when the three great bishops, Ridley, Latimer, and Cranmer were burned at the stake. Shortly after he was selected for the special duty of acting as escort to the young Princess Elizabeth, whom he brought to Rycote House on her journey to Woodstock, where she was to be detained as a state prisoner. This office might well have been the end of him when Elizabeth came to the throne, but his charm, hospitality and kindness only earned him her gratitude when she became Queen, for Lord Williams knew how to play his cards well.

And so on that autumn day in 1554, when she was only twenty-one, Elizabeth paid the first of many visits to her beloved Rycote; she had an even more special love when she was Queen for after Lord Williams's death it became the home of her dear 'owne crowe' (because of her dark complexion and black hair), the daughter of Lord Williams. She had married Henry Norreys, whose father, Sir Henry Norreys, accused of criminal intimacy with Anne Boleyn, had been executed on Tower Hill by Henry VIII, whose great consideration for Anne Boleyn was such that he allowed her head to be cut off with a sword instead of the customary axe. Though Elizabeth never mentioned her mother she had a special place in her heart for Henry Norreys, whom she later created Baron Norreys of Rycote. It was sufficient reason to bring her to Rycote five times, always in the autumn.

Six years were to pass before she made her second visit, then as Queen, bringing with her Robert Dudley, later Earl of Leicester, the reigning favourite and supposed murderer of his first wife, Amy Robsart, only two years previously. This rich, arrogant, handsome, extremely dangerous man did not endear himself at all to 'the crowe'. It was on this visit that, in a simple ceremony held in the garden of the house, the Queen knighted Henry Norreys. She came again in 1568 and 1570, creating him Baron Norreys in 1572. In this year she announced yet another visit in the autumn and great preparations were at once made to receive her. But on a dark and stormy night and very late, Leicester arrived alone, unwelcome, unexpected, unwanted, announcing the cancellation of the Queen's visit.

Lady Norreys, who had inherited all her father's ungovernable temper, refused to admit him to the house and told him 'to go sleep with his horse in the stables,' which the proud and angry Earl was forced to do. In spite of this gross injustice, for he had ridden hard from London to obey the Queen's orders, he came once again, and for the last time.

He had called at Rycote on his way to Kenilworth, and

there he wrote his last sad letter to his beloved Queen, with its postscript 'from your old lodging at Rycote'. When Elizabeth had read it she wrote on it 'his last letter' and put it away until her death. Some days after writing it Leicester himself was dead, having been confronted by the ghost of Amy Robsart, who warned him it would not be long before he joined her.

It was only quite recently that a lady, who was herself a psychic expert, came to Rycote and astonished the custodian by saying 'I have just seen my lord of Leicester.' It was the first time he had even heard of this new ghost, but it cannot be a surprise since Leicester had been so often there, happily and unhappily.

The Queen made her last visit to her beloved Rycote in the autumn of 1592, this time with her whole Court, a great and splendid occasion. None of them there could have guessed that within twelve years she herself, her host, her 'dear crowe' and their six sons would all be dead and that a splendid monument would be built in Westminster Abbey where Norreys and his wife would lie surrounded by the kneeling figures of their six sons. Though never seen by anyone, the ghosts must have been many to sadden that last occasion, for Lord Henry's eldest son was dead, his other sons were fighting for the Queen, Leicester was dead, and all remaining there were old.

Lord Norreys met his queen at the door with a gallant speech in which he said:

> I mean not to recount my service but to tell your Majesty that I am past all service save only devotion. My horse, my armour, my shield, my sword, the riches of a young soldier and an old soldier's relics I should here offer to your Highness, but my four boys have stolen them from me, vowing themselves to arms and leaving me to my prayers. This is my resolution and my desire that their lives should be employed wholly in your service and their deaths be their vows' sacrifice. Their deaths, the rumours

of which has so often affrighted the crow my wife that her heart has been as black as her feathers. I know not whether it be her affection or fondness but the crow thinketh her own birds the fairest because to her they are dearest, and although there be nothing more unfit to lodge your Majesty than a crow's nest yet shall it be most happy to us that it is by your Highness made a phoenix's nest.

There was music, dancing, feasting, gaiety and laughter, as well as happiness in each other, so precious was the friendship between subjects and sovereign. The next day in the rose garden, from each of the four corners, came messengers to the Queen, bearing letters and rich gifts from the four military brothers. Then once again, kneeling before his devoted sovereign, the old knight said, 'That my sons have remembered their duties it is my heart's comfort, that your Majesty accepteth them their hearts' heaven.' The next day she had gone, never to return, and once more the unseen ghosts came crowding back and took over the house, the rose garden, the deer park and the stables.

But there was one ghost seen for the first time and even then recorded, for in the house a monk had appeared, dressed in the brown habit of the Benedictine order, which the Queen's own father had so ruthlessly suppressed and driven into exile. Strange indeed it should have appeared at that very time and never departed since from the house where it once lived. He occupies one particular room in the present house, sometimes standing, but more often sitting on the bed. In World War II the house was used as a hospital for children, and the matron herself has recorded how she often saw him and that it became impossible to go upstairs to bed unless and until she had tapped on the door and said 'Good night, father!' She, of course, said nothing to any other member of her staff for fear of alarming them, and especially the children.

It was, therefore, all the more surprising when one day,

after the publication of his little book, in which Mr Morris related this story as told him by the matron, his telephone rang. It was one of the nurses who had served under this matron, had herself seen the monk many times, but also kept her secret for fear of alarming the others, not even telling matron. Though thirty years had passed it was a complete confirmation of the existence of the monk, who is now accepted as a more or less permanent guest who makes no demands on anyone at all.

In the year of James I's accession Rycote was inherited by Francis Norreys, grandson of the first baron, who was created a Knight of the Bath, Viscount Thame and Earl of Berkshire. After a life of debauchery, quarrelling and fighting he finally committed suicide in the park at Rycote by shooting himself wth a crossbow, his honours becoming extinct and only the barony of Norreys being inherited by his daughter. Her grandson was created Earl of Abingdon and in 1745 great sorrow fell on the family at Rycote when a terrible fire broke out and gutted the splendid Tudor mansion. Worse even than that was the death of the ten-year-old Lord Norreys, son and heir of the third Earl of Abingdon, who was burned to death in the fire.

The earl was so broken-hearted at this terrible tragedy that he could no longer continue living in the house he had loved so much, and where his young son had been born. He abandoned it utterly, having only some of the stones removed to Wytham, from which Berkshire village the Norreys family had originally come. The house eventually passed into private hands and remains today, skilfully and tastefully restored, and preserving what was left of the original mansion.

But who was Arabella? Her first recorded appearance was in 1645, and diligent research into Tudor costume has placed her in the period of Anne of Cleves, Jane Seymour, and even, except for the veil, the young Princess Elizabeth. Could it perhaps be Cicely Heron? Her father, Sir Thomas More, was often at Rycote, and his ghost has frequently been seen in the chapel where he assuredly worshipped when he stayed in the house. She certainly loved Rycote, and after the execution of first her father and then her husband, and the passing of the estate to Lord Williams of Thame, her grief must have been appalling. It seems so natural for her to be Arabella, searching for her loved ones and the home her husband had made so beautiful.

Or could it be Lord Williams's first wife Elizabeth? She it was who, together with her lord, entertained Henry VIII and Catherine Howard at Rycote shortly after they had bought the estate. There is a great deal of mystery about Elizabeth altogether, for she predeceased her husband by three years, when he married again; she lies buried in Rycote Chapel. Lord Williams died at Ludlow, but his body was brought to Rycote where he lay in great pomp and state before being buried in Thame church. Why then should the effigy of his first wife lie beside him and not his second? Why should they be facing west and not east, and why, anyway, was she not buried in Thame since her lord must have known he would himself be buried there?

It seems more likely, therefore, that she, who loved Rycote so dearly, entertained there so frequently, and bore her lord five children there, should be Arabella rather than Cicely Heron. One can only speculate. But for the veil it could even be the young Princess Elizabeth; and why not the Lady Margery Norreys herself? But whoever she may be they are waiting to see her again at Rycote, when the moon is full and the jewels she wears reflect the light, looking just as she did the last time. Though ghostly cold herself she can be assured of a warm welcome.

BATH

Perfumes and Mischief

One of the most curious things about the ghost life of Bath is that it is concentrated in two places, and even those adjoin each other. These ghosts have all been seen or heard, even smelt, a number of times by many different witnesses, who have all had their fair share of unease from the various ways ghosts have of expressing themselves. These have consisted of bumps, knocks, clashing of swords, perfumes and poltergeists; yet the result has never seemed to have caused fear, only astonishment and final acceptance that even glasses and cash registers should be hurled about.

Almost in the centre of the city stands the Theatre Royal; adjoining it and connected by a secret passage, now blocked up, is the Garrick's Head, named after the great eighteenth-century actor. This is the beautiful house built by Thomas Greenway in 1720 which so enchanted Beau Nash that he bought it and lived there for a great number of years, and frequently used it as a gaming house. It has been said also, though there is no proof at all, that he and his cronies used the secret passage as an escape route whenever his house was raided by the authorities.

Many strange noises have been heard in this passage, probably the ghosts of gamblers escaping from arrest, losers escaping from winners, drunk and quarrelsome gamblers fighting it out with their swords, or even bodies dumped there after being killed or wounded in duels, so prevalent at the time in England and especially in Bath.

Richard Nash, later called Beau Nash, was a very extra-

ordinary man. He was thirty-one when he came to Bath
in 1705, elegantly dressed, but with only enough money in
his pocket for a single night's lodging, determined to make
a mark on the city and a personal fortune out of gaming,
for he was a gambler of great skill. He was born in Wales;
he was sent down from Oxford for being secretly engaged
to a girl; he had entered the army, attracted by the prospect
of wearing a fine uniform and a sword, but hating the
discipline he discharged himself and went to study law in
the Inner Temple. While there he staged a pageant for
William III, which so pleased the King that he offered Nash
a knighthood. Nash, though thanking him and refusing the
honour, said he would prefer the money, but the monarch,
either pretending not to hear him or disliking what he had
heard, moved on. It was then that he took up gambling
seriously and with such skill that he decided to become
a professional. As Bath was at this time attracting most of
the nobility of England to take its waters and use its gaming
rooms, he decided to go there.

By singular good fortune, or by calculated design, he
managed to meet Captain Webster, who was frequently
drunk, was himself a gambler, and was also Master of
Ceremonies at the Assembly Rooms and the Pump Rooms.
Nothing might ever have come of this acquaintanceship had
not Captain Webster, after a furious and probably drunken
quarrel over a game of cards, been killed in the customary
duel. Almost before Bath was aware of it Nash slipped into
his place, earning the title of 'Beau' and 'the uncrowned king
of Bath'. His reign lasted for almost sixty years. He became
even more the Beau, distinguished by his fine clothes, tall
white beaver hat, brown curled wig, and elegant manners,
though physically he was not at all attractive. He travelled
everywhere in a magnificent sedan chair, or in a splendid
post chariot drawn by six dapple-grey horses, with postillions,

outriders, and French horns. In 1730 he bought the splendid house in St John's Court, now the Garrick's Head.

On Nash's arrival in Bath such was the state of the city that the corporation had actually been compelled to pass by-laws to prevent dogs, animals and even men from being thrown into the medicinal waters and defiling them. He immediately set about improving the standard of behaviour. He was strict about dress and forbade the wearing of top boots in the public rooms. He stopped the insulting behaviour of the chair-men, the wearing of swords, and thus duelling, having first proved his point by issuing a challenge himself and receiving a wound in the arm. He improved the streets and roads, compelled more lights to be used at night, tried his utmost to prevent young men from gambling while making a fortune at it himself, and was generous to a fault. Bath's debt to him is enormous and was expressed in a small pension in his last years, a lavish funeral, and a plaque on the wall of the house where he died in Sawclose which reads: 'In this house resided the celebrated Beau Nash and here he died February 1761.'

It was stopping the duelling which probably earned him the greatest praise, for at that time, in the reign of Queen Anne, swords were worn as an essential part of dress and indiscriminately drawn at the merest suggestion of a slight or insult, and most especially to settle a dispute at the card tables. It was normal for a person to be mortally wounded or killed for mere trifles, but most of all for cheating at cards. One loser who suspected cheating from his opponent drew his sword and pinned the man's hand to the card table until he confessed his fault. It became more and more serious until Beau Nash himself forbade it in his own recognised kingdom of Bath.

He had grown rich meanwhile from his gambling, but the Gaming Act of 1739 and the second one in 1745 prevented all games of hazard being played anywhere, and the decline in his fortunes was precipitous and final. He was forced to sell his beautiful house in St John's Court to pay his mounting debts, taking another and smaller one in Sawclose, the other side of the theatre. He then sold his unique collection of snuff boxes to buy food and firing, his coach and sedan chair had gone, and he lived in lonely misery on his memories at the age of eighty-five. At this point the Corporation of Bath granted him a pension of £10 a month and after his death voted that 'the funeral of Mr Nash be defrayed at a sum not exceeding fifty guineas'.

His body lay in state for four days and crowds filled the streets to see his splendid funeral cortège to Bath Abbey where he was buried. He himself would have greatly relished the pageantry, dirges, music, and the presence of the leading city mourners. It was, wrote a contemporary, 'just as when a real king dies, the people asking each other "Where shall we find such another?"' If any ghost has a right to haunt Bath it is his, yet he has never been seen, though his first fine house is haunted by other ghosts. Could the beau in Regency dress, often seen standing at the entrance to the theatre by actors coming and going over the years, be one of his friends? Surely it could not be the Beau himself? And could the person who is frequently seen and heard entering and leaving the passage, recognised by his boots, squeaking as if they were new and his brown curled wig falling over his shoulders, be one of his cronies? People who have seen this figure always assumed that he was one of the actors dressed for the play.

The really mysterious ghost is the Grey Lady. She has been seen more often than any of the others and as she haunts the theatre and is full of mischief the actors not only accept her but blame her for any odd things that go wrong. She likes to sit in the best box and watch the performance and has been known to cause a clock on the stage to strike at the wrong time or not to strike when it should and to perform various other little tricks. However as soon as she has pulled off one of her tricks she vanishes.

There is another woman ghost, far more sinister, who causes no pleasure, only eeriness. In the eighteenth century, in one of the grand rooms in Beau Nash's first house, now the public bar of the Garrick's Head, two men began to quarrel over a woman, each claiming her favours and completely disregarding the fact that her love for one of them was declared. The quarrel became violent and the quite un-willing lady who had become the stake in a terrible duel ran upstairs to her room. She crouched there, hearing the clash of swords and the oaths and shouts of the duellists, followed by a sudden silence as one lay dead. Next she heard the victor running up the stairs calling out her name to claim her. To her horror it was her lover who had been killed and in despair she flung herself out of the window and killed herself on the pavement below.

Over the years people have heard the clash of swords and the footseps of either the unhappy woman who had lost her lover, or the lover himself looking for her, but it is her ghost which has been seen in various parts of the house and not his. There is also the question of the smell of perfume in the bar cellar, an indefinable perfume which came and went even when no woman was there. Can this be her too, or the mischievous Grey Lady, and why was the perfume only smelt in the cellar? Who threw the glasses about the bar occasionally, and even caused the cash register to crash on the floor when only the landlord was there? Beau Nash himself would have approved of the perfume, but not the other activities in this once magnificent house; so perhaps after all it is his ghost that is moving about somewhere in the city which he loved so much.

CADBURY CASTLE

Camelot and Avalon

From its dominating position on a yellow limestone hill some twelve miles south-west of Glastonbury, South Cadbury Castle overlooks the whole Somerset countryside. Countless acres of green fields, banks, ditches, ramparts and marshes can be seen, where wild duck fly above the willows. It is a strange, mysterious, haunting countryside, which centuries ago was made up of vast swamplands and forests full of wild animals, its ancient fort a strong defensive earthwork camp.

Legends, folklore, and old customs still abound, and it is easy at certain times of the day, and assuredly at night, to imagine that any of them might be true. It was not at all surprising, therefore, that some forty years ago a visitor to these parts (by no means psychic) who had often stayed with her friend living near Cadbury Fort, saw a most beautiful house standing in a field. She had never noticed it on her previous visits and she began to go towards it. Before it stood a man and a little boy, both in costume of a period unknown to her, the boy much more richly dressed than the man.

Not able to believe her eyes but thinking they might be film actors, she continued walking towards them, her curiosity now fully aroused. To her amazement, they completely vanished. Upon returning home she told her hostess about the beautiful house she had seen and asked who owned it. She was told there was not, nor ever had been, such a house in that field. The visitor then described the man and boy dressed in costume, but her hostess said she had never heard of either in any local legend or story and that she must have imagined it all. The guest, still curious, returned next day to the field but there was no sign at all of any house, much less the figures of the man and a boy in costume.

By now deeply intrigued she went to the local and regional libraries, and after considerable research discovered that during the bloody wars between Stephen and the Empress Maud the boy Prince Henry, later Henry II, had been sent to Somerset for safety and to that very part where she had seen what was clearly his ghost. The house had belonged to one of his mother's loyal supporters, but its actual position had long been forgotten. This visitor had never at any time in her life been interested in this period of history and did not believe in ghosts, but now she had no doubt at all that she had seen not one but two, and with the apparition of a clearly defined house thrown in for good measure.

It is even more astonishing to know that towards the end of that same year, the hostess, who had found her guest's story so hard to believe, herself had a similar experience and it must be remembered that neither she nor her guest were psychic in any way. It was one dark Midsummer Eve when she and a companion were driving home after being out with friends. As they passed below Cadbury Fort the hostess saw to her astonishment a great number of glittering lights moving slowly down from the top of the hill to its base. Her companion said she could see nothing. As they drew nearer the bobbing, weaving lights grew brighter and clearer, and now before her astonished eyes she saw a column of men in armour on horseback. The lances they carried were tipped with bright flames and at the head of them all rode a man of immense stature and great dignity. In silence the column advanced and then vanished. There was now no doubt this phantom army could only be that described in the well-

94

known and centuries-old legend of King Arthur and his knights of the Round Table.

This ghostly army had been seen always on Midsummer Eve by people living in the nearby villages of North and South Barrow. Here also, they said, on the night of full moon the king led his band of knights with their glittering lance heads right round the hill before they stopped to water their horses at the nearby wishing-well and disappeared again into the hill.

Since Elizabethan times South Cadbury Castle had always been considered to be the site of Camelot, King Arthur's splendid palace which has now completely disappeared. Even in those times villagers spoke of it as the site of Arthur's Court and not as the grass-covered ramparts of what is thought to be an ancient British hill fort. They called it Arthur's Palace, as their ancestors had done since time immemorial. Quite near to it stood two small villages named West Camel and Queen's Camel, divided by the little river Cam on the banks of which a last terrible battle was once fought between King Arthur and Mordred, the knight who had betrayed him. Mordred was killed but not before wounding the king 'unto death'. Arthur's body was then carried down to the waiting barge where three queens wept in mourning, and he was borne to the Isle of Avalon at Glastonbury. In the abbey, together with his faithless wife Guinevere, he was laid to rest.

Evidence that two such places as Avalon and Camelot once existed in Somerset is also supported by the fact that a causeway once ran across the great marshes below the ramparts of the castle, marked on the map even today as 'King Arthur's Hunting Causeway'.

It is not then so difficult to disbelieve those who said that they had seen King Arthur at the head of his knights riding along the great causeway which bears his name and leads to

Avalon among the numerous scattered little islands of the
Somerset marshes. Many of these were skilfully reclaimed
by the monks when much later they built their great abbey
at Glastonbury. Ancient Britons, Celts, Romans, Saxons,
Picts and Danes have all fought and died there at the hands
of enemies who knew the marshes better than their invaders.
Even today vast tracts of the countryside remain as they
were centuries ago, and men are still unable to master them
completely. Above, and dominating almost the whole of
Somerset, proudly stands Glastonbury Tor, preserved forever
by the National Trust and probably its most sacred possession. It is said that beneath it lies buried in a stream or
spring the Holy Grail which Joseph of Arimathea brought
with him to England, and which was believed to be the
chalice used by Christ at the Last Supper.

The early monks of Glastonbury always believed in the
Arthurian legend, though no proof had ever been given.
Then in 1184 a raging fire broke out within the abbey,
destroying most of its precious relics and buildings as well
as the old church. Henry II gave a substantial sum of money
for rebuilding, the monks travelled many miles begging for
funds and such was their skill, determination and love for
their abbey that they virtually rebuilt it within two years.
Five years later they claimed to have discovered King
Arthur's grave, motivated it is said by King Henry II himself, who had once been told by a Welsh bard that the
legendary king was buried so deep that no Saxon would
ever discover him. When the monks began to excavate
they first found a stone then a lead cross with Latin letters
cut into the stone, which translated read: 'Here lies buried
the renowned King Arthur and Guinevere his wife in the
Isle of Avalon'. Deeper still they found a huge coffin made
from a hollow oak trunk, containing the bones of a strong
and extraordinarily large-boned man of great stature. At

the other end of the coffin lay a woman's skull encircled by 'a yellow tress of hair still retaining its colour and its freshness', but which crumbled to dust before the eyes of the wondering monks, who had at last proved their point to the unbelieving world.

In 1278, when Edward I and his queen visited the abbey, the remains of King Arthur and his wife were laid to final rest in a black tomb with a statue of the king at its foot and the original lead cross above it. The tomb was placed in the choir centre where, until Henry VIII dissolved the abbey, thousands of visitors came to pay homage to Arthur. Henry VIII ruthlessly pillaged the abbey, had its last abbot drawn through the streets on a hurdle and executed on the Tor, and ordered the complete demolition of the abbey so that the tomb disappeared with it.

It has been said that all these details of the discovery of Arthur's tomb were part of a great monastic fraud, but in 1902 archaeologists found the site of a grave, and later excavations have revealed the base of a shrine. In 1962 another grave site was discovered, whether or not it could be King Arthur's is open to doubt, but nothing of the Arthurian legend has diminished and indeed it has even been strengthened. In 1966 a serious attempt was made to prove that Cadbury Castle was in fact the legendary palace of the king and known as Camelot. The first members of the team who set out from Arthur's Well nearby were not only full of high hope and enthusiasm, but shared an absolute conviction that this would prove to be one of the most important archaeological excavations of all time, settling once and for all the old legend of 'the once and future king' who built his splendid palace there.

Strange legends have grown up throughout the centuries of history, so that it was not at all surprising when on the first day of the excavations one of the students was approached by a very old man who courteously, sincerely, and simply asked him: 'Have you come to take away our king?' The old man said he was one of many living in the villages below the hill on which the work was beginning who were convinced that this was what the archaeologists were doing. The old man then told how he and others had often seen strange visions there, particularly on Midsummer Eve, and repeated the story of the armed knights with their flaming lances and the immense figure of King Arthur at their head. They believed also, the old man continued, that Cadbury Castle was a hollow hill and that on St John's Eve the same procession issued through the golden gate within the hill which no one had ever found even after most diligent searching.

In Somerset, more than in any other part of England except Cornwall, the legends and beliefs surrounding Arthur are strongest, and in a strange and indefinable way, the lonely countryside gives credence to it all. Here Christianity first came to England when Joseph of Arimathea, who took Christ from his cross, brought the precious Holy Grail with him to Glastonbury and built the first Christian church in England of mud and wattle, upon which the great abbey of Glastonbury was built.

Many other counties have legends of Arthur, none more perhaps than Cornwall, who almost claim him for their own. In the castle of Sewingshields in Northumberland too, he and his faithless queen Guinevere who was seduced by his most dearly loved knight Sir Launcelot, together with all the knights, ladies and a pack of hunting hounds are said to lie buried in the vaults. In Richmond Castle, Yorkshire, they lie asleep waiting to be awakened by the blast of a horn, which lies on a table near the cave entrance, but which no one has ever dared to blow. In Wales and Scotland, in France, Italy and Sicily there are similar legends of a sleeping king waiting to be awakened when a country has reached its greatest crisis and most needs his help. This creative figure, be he real or not, has become a world legend. There are many who accept him as a reality and give cogent reasons and abundant evidence for his existence. Some say he lived in 410 AD, when the last Roman garrison was withdrawn from England to defend Rome against invasion when its great empire was crumbling away. After the departure of the legions England was wide open to all invaders and Angles, Jutes, Picts, Scots and Saxons came swiftly. It was then that King Arthur, with his famous black cavalry, rose to defend Britain against them, fighting battle after battle, gaining incredible victories, even crossing the seas and taking his armies into Europe, until he finally received his mortal wound in that terrible battle with Mordred.

Those first excavations at Cadbury Hill in 1966, however, gave no real evidence of the palace they sought, but it did reveal a Saxon wall of considerable thickness, shards of wine jars and dishes of Roman origin, and also the existence of an Iron Age ditch. The following year brought proof beyond all doubt that Cadbury Castle had been a sixth-century fort or stronghold built against Saxon invasion. Then a great trench was traced and excavated, which the archaeologists called 'the patio of King Arthur's palace'. In 1968 still further evidence supporting this new claim was revealed, for the trench was believed to be part of a foundation trench for a large sixth-century hall or palace about thirty-five feet wide and seventy feet long. This could well have been the Great Hall of Camelot where King Arthur held his court of knights, and which the archaeologists had sought since they first began to excavate.

The only wonder is that the king's ghost does not haunt the abbey ruins, but then perhaps it does. Whether one does or does not believe in any of the legends associated with the abbey ruins, the story of Arthur has been and still is for people all over the world, a beautiful one, so may we not all be the richer for that?

The late Sir Winston Churchill summed it up in his brilliant and masterly manner in *History of the English Speaking Peoples*:

> If we could see exactly what happened we should find ourselves in the presence of a theme as well-founded, as inspired, and as inalienable from the inheritance of mankind as the Odyssey or the Old Testament. It is all true, or it ought to be, and more and better besides. And wherever men are fighting against barbarism, tyranny, and massacre, for freedom, law and honour, let them remember that the frame of their deeds, even though they themselves be exterminated, may perhaps be celebrated as long as the world rolls round.

LITTLECOTE

The Manor House murder

It was a wild winter night in 1575 and every cottage door was shut in the little Berkshire village of Great Shefford, some three or four miles from the Wiltshire border. No one was more glad to be indoors than old Mother Barnes, the greatly respected and much needed midwife. She had had her usual day of care and trouble with babies born, being born, and to be born, so that a sudden violent knocking on her door did nothing to gladden her heart. As she hesitated the knocking grew more urgent, and moving across the room she opened the door. Standing there in the pouring rain were two saddled horses and two men she had never seen before. Curtly and harshly one of them ordered her to pack her things and come at once to a lady who was in heavy labour, but that she must come blindfolded so that she could not identify the lady or the house to which she must go. The situation was dramatic and unpleasant and though all her instincts warned her not to go Mother Barnes had no alternative, for the men were threatening and already seizing and blindfolding her. She was helped to mount pillion behind one of the men and all three rode away.

The rain was drenching down and a high wind blew across the bleak Berkshire downs so that even had the horsemen said anything she could not have heard. The roads were narrow, sodden and bumpy, and did nothing at all to ease the journey which continued for some time. When they reached their destination she was bluntly told to dismount. Someone at the door took her hand and from that moment Mother Barnes kept a cool head and began to count the number of rooms through which she passed and the steps up which presently she was led. All of these details were so accurate in the evidence she later gave that the house was easily identified though at the time she had no idea whatsoever that it was Littlecote in Wiltshire. The deposition she gave, when no longer able to keep her secret of all that happened on that terrible night was faithfully recorded by Anthony Bridges, the local magistrate to whom she went. However, accounts of this story differ in details.

> They broughte her unto a fayre house and alighted her neere a doore of the said house at the wch doore one of those that broughte her made some little noyse, eyther by knockinge or rynginge of some belle, whereupon ther came to the said doore a tall, slender gentleman, having uppon hym a longe gowne of blacke velvett, and bringinge a light with hym, who so soone as she was entred into the said doore, made faste the same, and shutt out those that broughte her, and presently broughte her upp a stayres into a fayre and large great chambre, being hanged all aboute with arras, in the wch chambre there was a chymney, and therein was a great fyre and from thence through the said chambre she was conveyed into another chambre of leeke proportion and hanged in leeke sorte as the fyrste was, in the wch chambre was also a chymney, and a great fyre, and passinge through the said seconde chambre, she was broughte into a thyrde chambre, hanged also rychlye with arras, in the wch chambre there was a bed rychlye and gorgeouslye furnished, the curteynes of the said bed beinge alle close drawn about the said bed. And as soone as she was entred in at the said doore of the laste resited chambre, the said partye in the longe velvett gowne ronned softlye in her eare sayinge; 'loe in younder bed lyeth the gentlewoman that you are sente for to come unto, go unto her and see that you doe youre uttermoste endevoyre towards her, and yf she be safely delivered you shall not fayle of greate rewarde; but if shee myscarry in her traveyle you shall dye.

The man that the now terrified Mother Barnes stood before was 'Wild' Darrell, so-called for his drunken, dissolute ways, his ruthlessness, and cruelty. John Aubrey, the inimit-

able diarist and gossip, who once saw a portrait of him
described him as: 'a huge ugly man, whose wife, in his
frequent absences from Littlecote would have all the women
of the country thither and make them drunk as she would
be herself'.

Anthony Bridges continues:

Whereuppon, as one amased, she departed from the said gentleman to the beddes syde, fyndynge there a gentlewoman in traveyle,
lyinge in great estate, as by the furniture uppon and aboute her
it dyd appear, this gentlewoman's face beinge covered eyther with
a viser or a cell, (a mask) and shortly after her comynge she was
delivered of a man childe, who for lacke of other clothes, was
fayne to be wrapped in the mid-wyfe's apron, and so was carried
by the said mid-wyfe into one of the two fyrste chambres that
she passed throughe at the fyrste, finding the said gentleman there
at her coming thither, whoe demanded of her whether the partye
that shee came from was delivered of childe or noe, whoe
answered that she was safely delivered of a man child wch shee
there presently shewed him, requirynge him that some provision
of clothes might be had to wrap it with alle, who incontinentally
broughte her to the fyre side into wch he commanded her to caste
the childe, whereupon shee kneeled downe unto him, desirynge
him that he would not seeke to destroy it but rather give it
unto her, promisinge to keep it as her owne, and to be sworne
never to disclose it, the wch thinge the gentleman woulde not
yeld unto, but forthwith the childe was caste into the fyre, but
whether by the mid-wyfe herselfe, or by them both I doe not
perfectly remembre, and so soone as this horrible facte was done
she was commanded to goe backe again to the gentlewoman,
where she remayned all that day and by nighte was broughte
back agayne by those two men that broughte her thither, whoe
sett her some myles distante from her house, but whether two
myles or more I doe not remembre.

These were the bare, grim details of a story Mother Barnes
kept secret for no less than fourteen years, before finally
confessing all she had seen and heard that terrible night.
The name of the gentlewoman she delivered of a son has
never been recorded, only that she died about a week later.
The original bed and curtain from which Mother Barnes so

astutely cut a damning piece of evidence, were bought and taken away some years ago by an American, but the landing and the bedroom have been haunted ever since either by the woman who died there, or by Mother Barnes or Wild Darrell or all three. Certainly the ghost of Mother Barnes, or so it is believed by her shape and period clothes, has been seen quite recently in the grounds. The ghost of Wild Darrell has also been seen at Great Shefford, still uneasily pursuing the woman he so brutally treated and the babe he murdered. It is said that blood-stains used to appear mysteriously in the haunted chamber at the same time as the ghost of the distracted midwife carrying the babe in her arms was seen. It is also said that the floor of the bedroom where Darrell walks can never be kept in repair, no matter how often and how well it is treated, but constantly moulders away.

When all the evidence of the midwife's deposition had been sifted and carefully examined it was decided that the unknown house could only be Littlecote, and if there ever had been any doubt at all about her statements it was totally disproved by the discovery in the chamber she had so accurately described, of the hole, cut out of the bed hangings, into which the piece Mother Barnes had taken fitted perfectly. It was on this evidence alone that Wild Darrell was arrested and brought to trial, though subsequent details of this are more than confusing. John Aubrey says he was brought before Sir John Popham, then Attorney General, and that this judge 'had the noble house, park and manor and I think more for a bribe to save Dayrell's life'. The verdict was certainly *Nolle Prosequi*, and it is certain that Darrell made over Littlecote three years before his death to Sir John Popham.

The intriguing story came to the ears of Sir Walter Scott, who in his novel *Rokeby* wrote a ballad of the whole story

related to him by Lord Webb Seymour, though Scott's version
is as vague and as far from the truth as his version of the
murder of Amy Robsart in his novel *Kenilworth*. An
important letter, also dealing with the Littlecote murder,
was discovered by Canon Jackson at Longleat, written to Sir
John Thynne from Sir Henry Knyvett:

> Syr, I beseech you let me crave so much favour of you as to
> procure your servant Mr Bonham most effectively to examine his
> sister tochinge her usage at William Darrell's, the birth of her
> children, howe many they were and what became of them. She
> shall have no cause off fear trulie to confes the uttermost; for I
> will defend her from all parell how so ever the case fall owte.
> The brute of the murder of one of them increaseth fowlely, and
> theare falleth owte such other heyghnous matter against him as
> well took him to the quick . . . From Charlton this 11th January
> 1578 your loving friend H Knyvett.

Much later a commentator added that it was a pity the
letter was not printed in full 'as neither Sir H. Knyvett nor
Sir John Thynne were above suspicion'.

In point of fact though Wild Darrell was never punished
for this monstrous crime his death was as violent as any to
which he might have been condemned, for he was thrown
from his horse and broke his neck in Littlecote Park three
years after his trial. The place where he fell is also haunted,
for it was said that the cause of his death was his horse
shying in the twilight at the sudden apparition before them
both of a child all on fire and in flames. The place is known
today as 'Darrell's Stile'. The Darrell line ceased with this
death of one of the more unsavoury of Elizabethan characters.
Amongst Darrell's many mistresses was his own sister, who
was even held to be the incestuous mother of the child
burned in the fire. In 1823 the *Gentleman's Magazine* said of
Littlecote:

> In the dusk the country people have often seen in the avenue
> to the house a coach curiously drawn by six horses, in which

are a gentleman and a lady richly dressed, a child of angelic
beauty on her lap, but both the gentleman and lady were headless.

There was a very strange variation of the notorious Little-
cote murder. On 2 April 1601 William Knyght resided at
Hanover and wrote to an unknown correspondent 'that one,
Hugh Broughton had been making monstrous speeches of
Queen Elizabeth, not having been rewarded by her for his
trouble.' He declared:

> That Her Majesty had a daughter, also that she had been of long
> time past married to Lord Chancellor Hatton had not Mrs
> Ratcliffe hindered it. Also it is true one McDorell sent to a
> midwife in London who was driven in a coach by sundry ways to
> a palace at Hampstead (Marshall); and the midwife, being carried
> up to a secret chamber, where a lady lay in travail, was com-
> manded to do her best and preserve the lady, whatsoever became
> of the child; and after being delivered of a daughter, she was
> brought to another chamber where was a very great fire of coals,
> into which she was commanded to cast the child, and so it was
> burnt. This midwife was rewarded with a handful of gold, and
> at her departure, one came to her with a cup of wine, and said,
> Thou whore, drink before thou goest from hence, and she drank,
> and was sent back to her house, where within six days after she
> died of poison, but revealed this before her death; all which he
> insinuated to be done for Her Majesty.

Littlecote, between Ramsbury in Wiltshire and Hungerford in Berkshire, was built between 1490 and 1520 by the
Darrells, who in 1415, through marriage into the Calston
family, inherited the manor and its house. It was this family
which built the most splendid 110ft Long Gallery, also
haunted. All the splendid state rooms were built on the
first floor, but the finest individual feature of the whole house
is the magnificent Cromwellian Chapel, built much later
and probably the only complete example of its kind in
England. Its black pews, linen-fold panelling, high dominating pulpit from which three-hour sermons were preached,

the domestic staff having to stand all that time at the back of the chapel, is a grim reminder of those joyless, musicless days. It was along the gallery high above this chapel, which leads to the haunted landing and chamber, that the bewildered Mother Barnes was led on that fateful night. The Pophams held possession of Littlecote until 1922 when Sir Ernest Wills, the tobacco magnate, bought it and in whose family it still remains. It is open to the public, and visitors flock here from all over England.

Littlecote, an exquisite Tudor manor house approached along a drive of young and carefully pruned limes, is a unique example of its kind. It stands serene amidst its spacious and beautiful lawns and gardens, through which a trout stream flows; gardens which seem to extend far into the lush green Kennet countryside surrounding the house. Its façade of small Tudor red bricks, mellowed by centuries of time to a most pleasing colour, its Cotswold stone roofs, its mullioned windows, Tudor doorways and chimneys, are as lovely a sight as any in England. It seems impossible, sitting by the flowing trout stream backed by flowers, musk, bul-rushes and sweet smelling shrubs, that a place of such calm and beauty could possibly be haunted; yet it is, if the stories are to be believed, and quite recently ghosts have been seen both inside and outside the house.

In 1947 both Sir Edward and Lady Wills saw and heard a ghost coming along the Long Gallery. It was of a lady carrying a light which cast a shadow over the ceiling as she moved. Not very tall, it was fair-headed and wore a pink nightdress. Sir Edward actually followed it as it did some-thing ghosts rarely do, that is to open the door of the room into which it was entering. Sometimes, terrifying screams have been heard from the haunted landing and bedroom where the murder took place. Other ghosts have been seen by various official guides to the house, one of which is said to be that of Mrs Leybourne Popham, a most beautiful woman according to her portrait in the house, who haunts the garden although no reason has ever been given for her doing so.

As if this were not enough for one house, there is an even stranger ghost, sinister and limping. During the 1920s one of the most notorious swindlers the City has ever produced, Gerard Lee Bevan, who had all Wild Darrell's ruthlessness and total disregard for other people, though nothing of his criminal tendencies, became a tenant of Littlecote. An Eton and Oxford education might have produced a better product, so also might his descent from a family of bankers, but all it did was to make him a quite outstanding financial swindler. He was arrogant enough to catch any train from Paddington and pull the communication cord at Hungerford where, after paying the £5 fine, he would join his chauffeur in a waiting car. Success after success went to his head and quite late in his life, when he was about fifty, he began to drink and pay attention to women. He became chairman of the giant City Equitable Fire Insurance Company, and director of many other companies, highly trusted and respected for his financial astuteness by all who knew him.

In the early part of 1922 his giant insurance company crashed, and the losses of this and his other companies totalled some £4,000,000. Bevan had escaped to Paris the night before with a woman friend and evaded the police everywhere by posing as an artist. He was eventually caught at Innsbruck, betrayed by a so-called woman friend, arrested, brought to England and sentenced to seven years' imprisonment. After his release he went to Havana, where he died at the age of sixty-nine, leaving millions of ruined shareholders throughout the country. It should be the ghosts of these bankrupted unfortunates looking for their lost money who haunt Littlecote, but it is not, for a psychic expert recently identified the ghost of a limping man. Bevan limped in more ways than one.

As one goes away from Littlecote, serenely set like a jewel in its lush green meadows, smooth lawns, and beautiful gardens, one wonders how even the unhappiest ghost could not find peace at last here. Yet there they are still, all restlessly moving about the place, even after nearly 400 years of bondage.

Just to finish off the story there is said to be yet another ghost, Sir John Popham himself, though not at Littlecote but at Park Farm, south-west of the Brendon Hills in Somerset, near Wellington. Here he is said to have crawled out of Hell and now to be making his way to the family vault in Wellington church, but only by one cock's stride a year. Since he died in 1607 it is going to take a long time to get there. It is said that he did in fact reach a certain farm but that his ghost haunted the farmer so much that he called in a witch to exorcise it. The witch cast a spell on Sir John and sent him back to the pit from which he first crawled, so that he had to start his journey all over again. One wonders whether the possession of Littlecote was worth all that.

LONGLEAT

Ghosts Galore

The immense Italian-style mansion of Longleat in Wiltshire, home of the Marquess of Bath, standing within its 11,000 acres of parkland and lakes, is said to be the most haunted stately home in England. In spite of many attempts over the years to dispel these theories, to allay suspicion, and finally to call in psychic experts to verify the existence of the ghosts, they continue to flit about the house. They are to be found in Green Lady's Walk, Stable Courtyard, Bishop Ken's Library, the Red Library, and in the corridors and passages. Legend also has it that the house and family will be finally doomed if the swans fly away and never return to the Longleat lakes where they have nested for centuries.

In 1916, the wife of the fifth Marquess of Bath, who was herself psychic, suddenly saw from her window five swans flying very low and heading for the house, coming nearer and nearer, before one of them suddenly flew away from the others, leaving them to return to the lake whilst he disappeared into the distance. She told her family that this was a bad omen and that she feared for the life of her eldest son, Viscount Weymouth, who was fighting in France. The very next day a telegram was brought to her announcing his death in action.

Later still she asked why there were men working on the roof and why dust sheets were over the floors and furniture of the Hall, but no one had seen or heard anything at that time. The whole incident came back with force when shortly after, fire broke out in the roof, severely damaging it, so that workmen had to go up to carry out repairs and therefore covered everything below with dust sheets.

Of all the ghosts at Longleat the kindliest must surely be that of Sir John Thynne, 'the Builder', the recognised head of the great line, who haunts the Red Library. He it was who first conceived Longleat when in 1540, for the sum of £53, he bought the Augustinian priory which had been occupied by the Black Canons for over 250 years until the Dissolution of the Monasteries, and as so often happened, collected many monkish curses into the bargain. Sir John was a great favourite of the Protector, the Duke of Somerset, who knighted him, but after the Duke's fall from power both he and Sir John were imprisoned in the Tower, the latter being released on payment of £6,000. In 1567 the old house on which he had spent so much time and money was burned down and he at once started to build the present Longleat. He supervised every single detail so thoroughly and so accurately that the actual work and name of the architect he employed has almost gone into oblivion.

It was one of the first great mansions to be built in the new Italian fashion so much liked by Henry VIII, and it had no less than 100 rooms, lavishly furnished, below which were huge cellars. The early formal gardens merged perfectly into the surrounding countryside. Thynne hired Scottish freemasons to do the work, and as they were unable to hold services because there was no Presbyterian chapel he allowed them to build one at Horningsham nearby, the earliest in England and still used. He also employed the celebrated plasterer Charles Williams. For reasons best known to himself he tried hard to prevent Queen Elizabeth I coming to visit him, but finally yielded to Court pressure and received her on one of her Progresses, to their mutual pleasure. His reluctance might well have been a question of expense, for with the Queen's varied tastes, her love of food and hunting, her vast retinue of servants, she very often bankrupted her many hosts. Throughout twelve long years he closely watched the progress of his beloved house take shape in stone exactly as he wished, but died in 1580 before its completion. It is pleasing to think that his quiet and gentle ghost comes back again and again, probably to be reassured that everything is still all right after nearly 400 years.

Curiously enough there is a second library and a second ghost, another kindly one at that. At the top of the house is Bishop Ken's Library, where at midnight on the anniversary of his death in 1711, the gentle bishop returns to his beloved library in which he wrote most of his hymns and *Divine Poems*. He might well have ended his clerical career even earlier than he did, for when he was at Winchester he refused to allow Nell Gwynne lodgings in the cathedral close. In spite of every possible advice and even pressure from Court circles, he was a man of the strictest morals and beliefs and would not yield. When Charles II was informed he made no comment at all and seemed to be rather indifferent. Later, however, when the bishopric of Bath and Wells fell vacant, he asked one of his counsellors: 'Where is that good little man who refused his lodging to poor Nell?' So the daring and unyielding bishop was appointed Bishop of Bath and Wells, to his delight. This was not only a valuable preferment but Longleat which was in his diocese was owned by the first Viscount Weymouth, who had been his closest friend since their Oxford days together.

In 1688 Ken was sent to the Tower with six other bishops by James II for refusing to publish the king's Declaration of Indulgence. All seven were tried and acquitted to the joy of the public. He next refused to take the oath to William and Mary since his conscience told him he had already done so to James II, even though he was bitterly opposed to Roman Catholicism, and for this he was deprived of his bishopric. It was then that Viscount Weymouth came forward and offered him a home and hospitality at Longleat for as long as he liked. Thus it was that the bishop came to live there and remained for no less than twenty years in that sanctuary which he made his own, and which still bears his name, and dedicated one of his books of poems in gratitude and affection to the Viscount. Incidentally it was this Viscount who first had brought to Longleat the pine from North America known thereafter as the famous Weymouth Pine. It was his successor, the second Viscount, who called in 'Capability' Brown to lay out the immense landscape gardens one sees today at Longleat.

If ever there should have been a really good ghost at Longleat it would have been that of Thomas Thynne, known all over England as 'Tom of Ten Thousand' because that was his vast annual income in those days. He was a close friend of the highly untrustworthy and potentially dangerous Duke of Monmouth, supposed bastard of Charles II, and Lucy Walter, whom Nell Gwynne dubbed 'Prince Perkin', after the other imposter of that name. During one of his visits to Longleat the Duke spoke of the richest and most sought after heiress in England, Lady Elizabeth Ogle, and promised his influence in promoting a marriage between her and Thomas Thynne. She was the daughter of the eleventh Earl of Northumberland, and the widow, at fourteen, of the Earl of Ogle, heir to the Duke of Newcastle, who died a year later. Nothing suited the prodigal and extravagant Thynne more, and because of his great wealth the proposal was at once approved and he became betrothed to this young red-headed and spirited beauty. He began to prepare for her coming to Longleat as his wife, spending vast sums of money on splendid apartments and furniture, sparing nothing for such a bride. But Lady Elizabeth was mature enough at fifteen to have had more than enough of one marriage and after the wedding she fled to Holland before her second marriage was even consummated. A notorious young adventurer, more of a pirate than a gentleman, called Count Charles John Konigsmark, who had fallen deeply in love with her when he was in England, followed in hot pursuit. Since he was a man who had no scruples and could not conceive of any possibility of not having whatever he desired in life, he could see no other way of obtaining his loved one but to murder Thomas Thynne. He hired assassins and sent them to England to do the job, following later himself to see it was thoroughly carried out.

The three ruffians he hired were an impoverished Pole named Boroski, a Captain Vratz, and a Lieutenant Stern, all types of mercenary adventurers who wandered about Europe picking up what they could in the way of money by any means, even if it were as unsavoury as this venture. Once in London they began to study Thomas Thynne's every movement throughout the day and into the night, for his life had a regular pattern of social comings and goings. Quite often he went to the house of the Dowager Countess of Northumberland whose granddaughter had been his wife for so brief a time. She lived near St James's Palace, and he was obliged to go along Pall Mall, then a mere lane, to reach her house. On a dark Sunday night in February 1682, the assassins saw his coach leaving the Countess's house, and rode after him. Coming alongside, Stern pulled up in front of the coach while Vratz threatened the driver with a pistol. Boroski, in cold blood, pushed his blunderbuss into the coach and against Thynne's body, firing five bullets point blank into it after which all three rode away leaving the man dying. He did not die until a few hours later but the linkmen had already raised the alarm. The Duke of Monmouth was the first to arrive and stayed with him until the end.

A reward of £200 was immediately offered for apprehension of the assassin, a considerable sum of money in those days, and an informer at once gave Gibbons, one of the Duke of Monmouth's retainers, information which led to Konigsmark's arrest as he tried to embark, disguised, on a ship. He at once denied the charge or any knowledge of the murder and was tried and acquitted by a bribed jury. This jury did, however, bring in a verdict of guilty against the three hired assassins, who were all executed. Vratz requested to be embalmed and his body to be placed on view to the public for fifteen days after his death. Konigsmark, after his sensational trial, fled to the continent and was killed fighting in Greece four months later.

Lady Elizabeth Ogle took Charles Seymour, sixth Duke of Somerset as her third husband. She became a close friend of Queen Anne, a political figure to be reckoned with, and also an implacable enemy of Dean Swift. She was furiously angry for the rest of her life at a cynical and bitter lampoon Swift wrote which contained the following cruel lines:

> And dear England, if ought I understand,
> Beware of CARROTS from NORTHUMBERLAND;
> Carrots sown THYNN a deep root may set
> If so they be in SOMER-SET.
> Their CUNNINGS-MARK thou for I have been told,
> They assassin when young, and poison when old.

She had her revenge for when Swift's nomination came up for the bishopric of Hereford, which he much coveted, she easily persuaded the queen to pass him over.

There are other ghosts, one in a linen cupboard and one in the Stable Courtyard, which is part of the servants' wing. The latter is an unknown but very real ghost who knocks on the door of a certain bedroom and has been seen and felt in the corridor. But the strongest one of all, and the most feared, is the celebrated ghost of the corridor known as Green Lady's Walk.

Thomas Thynne, second Viscount Weymouth, whose son was created first Marquess of Bath, was not in the direct succession line, and for some very peculiar reason disliked the inherited Longleat from the start. He was born posthumously and was twenty-one before he came to live there. He left it almost at once to go and live in a small manor house in the nearby village of Horningsham, where the first Sir John Thynne had allowed his Scottish freemasons to build the Presbyterian chapel when he was building Longleat. His portrait suggests that he was not a very clever man, with a vicious face, and this accurately reflects his subsequent actions. He married twice, taking for his second wife the beautiful Lady Louisa Carteret, daughter of the Earl of Granville. His bride was universally admired for her great beauty and charm. These are evident in the portrait in the dining room where she is shown wearing the beautiful green dress which gave its name to the haunted corridor and to a scandalous legend which was known all over London at that time.

It would seem that the Viscount was quite unpopular, for Sarah, Duchess of Marlborough expressed her astonishment that Lady Louisa should have married such a man. His strange behaviour was noticed in his own village, and he seems to have had an inexpressible dislike for tradition and for big and costly houses. It is said that the real reason he did not choose to live at Longleat was because his stepfather, Lord Lansdowne, came to stay there. He remained so long that the Viscount was able to use his continued presence in the house as an excuse, saying that as one of them had to go, he would leave himself and he never returned to live at Longleat.

His second marriage turned out to be as miserable as his first. It was not at all surprising that the beautiful Lady Louisa met a dashing young man with whom she at once fell in love and he with her. To make it easier for both of them she hid her lover at Longleat until her husband discovered him. A savage duel took place up and down the corridor, finally ending in the death of the lover, whose body the Viscount buried under the cellar flagstones. Some 250 years later, when central heating was first installed at Longleat, the body of a man was certainly found under the cellar floor. The body crumbled away as soon as it was exposed to air, leaving only the jackboots he was wearing at the time. The corridor where the fatal duel took place is haunted by the unhappy Lady Louisa. Her spirit walks up and down in terrible grief for her dead lover, and because of the colour of her dress the place has always been called 'Green Lady's Walk'.

Since it was first opened to the public, millions of people have come to visit and enjoy Longleat's lovely house and grounds. It is to be hoped that the swans will never bring the prophesied doom to this ancient family and beautiful house.

TIDWORTH

The demon drummer

Just over the Hampshire border in Wiltshire is the village of
North Tidworth. It is some ten miles from Andover and
nine from Amesbury. Once a year it puts on such a splendid
and colourful military tattoo that people come in their
thousands to see and hear it. It is not surprising that there
are military ghosts to be found here. One is said to be of
a Highlander in full dress, playing his pipes; another, of a
Roman soldier which must therefore be about the oldest
ghost in England. In the British Museum there is a Roman
pavement excavated at Tidworth in 1836, so it may well be
that there is a phantom soldier still looking for it.

At the adjacent village of South Tidworth there is a
far more famous military ghost, as well documented and
disturbing as any in the country. So much excitement did
the story of its activities cause at the time that Charles II
immediately ordered a Royal Commission to go down to
Tedworth, as it was then called, and make the fullest possible
investigations. Their journey was a sheer waste of time as
the examiners, who were probably all non-psychic, witnessed
no manifestations whatsoever, either by day or by night.
The commissioners returned to London, unable to make any
constructive report and the whole matter was dropped.

When a certain Dr Joseph Glanvil went to make personal
investigations things were very different indeed. A whole
series of disturbing incidents took place round a central
figure known to this day as 'The Demon Drummer of Tedworth'. Glanvil gave a long and meticulously detailed account
of every one of these almost incredible events, finally publish-

ing them in a long article entitled *Saducismus Triumphatus*. It is an astonishing narration of poltergeist activities, and one wonders how all the people involved not only continued to live there for as long as they did but managed to keep their sanity at all.

On a day in March, 1661, a certain Wiltshire magistrate named Mr John Mompesson was on business in the neighbouring town of Ludgershall when he heard the continual beating of a drum. As this was invariably used to announce some important proclamation he sent for the local bailiff and asked him what all the drum beating was about. To his astonishment the bailiff told him that for some days now the town had been troubled by this drummer. He was a vagrant and as such had also demanded money from the local constable by producing a signed pass which the constable suspected was a counterfeit one. Mr Mompesson then told the bailiff to bring the drummer before him for questioning and verification of his pass. When the drummer, whose name was William Drury, was brought before him and asked why he was disturbing the peace of the town, he replied that he had every right to play his drum since he had a warrant entitling him to do so. Accordingly, he produced his pass and the accompanying warrant. Mr Mompesson saw at once that the signatures were forgeries. He ordered the drummer there and then to take off his drum and the bailiff to charge the constable to take the drummer before the next Justice of the Peace for further examination and punishment.

The drummer, seeing his cause was lost, admitted the warrant had been forged but earnestly pleaded with the magistrate to let him keep his drum. His plea was refused but Mr Mompesson agreed he should have it restored to him if his previous conduct and character proved to be good. Meanwhile the bailiff was ordered to keep the drum and to place the drummer in charge of the constable.

It seems that between then and April, the next month, when Mr Mompesson had departed for London, the drummer had wheedled the bailiff into releasing him. For some inexplicable reason the bailiff had returned the drum to Mr Mompesson's house. Now the real trouble began, for upon his return from London the magistrate found his wife terrified by what she thought were thieves trying to break into the house, 'so much so that the house was like to have been broken up'. Three days later, when the magistrate himself had gone to bed, there was a tremendous knocking on the door and weather-boarding of the house. Taking up his brace of pistols Mr Mompesson at once got up and opened the door. The knocking began again at another door, then another, and as he went round the house it became louder, and loudest of all on the roof. The magistrate saw nothing at all and returned to his room mystified and greatly disturbed. From that time onwards these noises became alarmingly frequent whenever he and his wife were going to sleep, sometimes continuing for five nights in succession followed by a break of perhaps three days before starting again.

After a moneths disturbance without (writes Glanvil) it came into the Room where the Drum lay, four or five nights out of seven within half an hour after they were in bed, continuing almost two hours. The sign of it just before it came was, they still heard an hurling in the Air over the house, and at its going off, the beating of a Drum like that at the breaking up of a Guard. It continued in this room for the space of two moneths, which time Mr Mompesson himself lay there to observe it. Mrs Mompesson being brought to bed there was but little noise the night she was in Travail nor for any three weeks afterwards till she had recovered strength, but after this civil cessation it returned in a ruder manner than before and following and vexing the other young children, beating their bedsteads with that violence. For an hour together it would beat Roundheads, Cuckolds, the Tattoo, and several other parts of war as well as any Drummer.

It was following this cessation that the evil spirit, for such it was now considered to be, seemed to concentrate on the children, shaking their beds, scratching under them, following them from one room to another. Mr Mompesson had by then discovered a cockloft in the house under the roof which never seemed to be troubled, and so the children were put to bed there, but no sooner were they asleep than the knockings and disturbances started all over again.

Throughout the whole of Glanvil's narrative it seems almost inconceivable that any parents, even in those days, could allow their children to be so consistently and cruelly terrified. It says much for the stupidity of the magistrate that he continued to keep his children there especially as it seems evident that he was himself interested in manifestations and the occult.

On 5 November 1662 'it kept a mighty noise', and a servant entering the frightened children's room saw two floor boards moving.

> He at once boldly commanded the spirit to bring one to him which it did to within a yard of where he stood. Whereupon he said: 'Nay, let me have it in my hand', whereupon it was shoved right home to him so up and down and to and fro some twenty times till Mr Mompesson forbade his servant so much familiarity. This was in the daytime and seen by a whole roomful of people. That morning it left a sulphorous smell behind it which was very offensive.

The poltergeist then began to work in earnest, for porringers, plates, bedclothes, books, shoes, all were hurled about the room at odd moments of the day and night. It got so serious that Mr Mompesson called in the local minister, Mr Craig, to endeavour to exorcise the spirit. He knelt down by the bed where the children lay and proceeded to pray very earnestly, but was rudely rewarded by chairs, shoes, clothes and furniture being hurled about the room and 'being struck on the leg by a bedstaff but so favourably that a lock of wool could not have fallen more softly'. It was only then that the obdurate Mr Mompesson decided the children should be sent away from the house to a neighbour, all except his eldest daughter, aged ten, whom he took into his own chamber which had been perfectly quiet for a whole month. That very night the drummer began his tattoo all over again just as he had done up and down the street in Ludgershall where Mr Mompesson had first heard him. The most incredible feature of this whole story is the magistrate's inability to associate the drumming with the drum still lying in his house where the bailiff had unaccountably sent it.

As the neighbours in charge of the children had other visitors they were obliged to send the children back to their father. The parlour had been almost totally free of disturbance for some time so they were put there to sleep, but once again the drumming and the poltergeist began. There was so much noise caused by these activities that it was heard a good way away, causing such gossip that the Royal Commission came to investigate.

Towards the end of December, 1662 the noises took a new turn, becoming now a constant jingling of money, a new and quite unfamiliar, although less terrifying disturbance. Now the Tidworth people began not only to suspect but openly to accuse Mr Mompesson of practising witchcraft. This was a serious crime indeed in those days and punishable even by death in some cases, but the charges were most vehemently and indignantly denied by the magistrate. The jingling of money eventually ceased and the spirit returned to torment the children. Among other things it threw Mrs Mompesson's mother's bible into the ashes of the fire, though now it made no noise. Then one night it switched its attack from the children to one of the servants, holding him down in his bed, throwing his shoes at his head, pulling his bedclothes away from him in the night, and only finally desisting when the furious servant drew his sword and began attacking the spirit wherever he felt it might be. It became clear that whenever he did draw his sword he was thereafter left in peace.

About the beginning of 1663 'they were wont to hear a singing in the chimney before it came down'. Lights were seen moving about the house from room to room, footsteps were heard up and down the stairs and the maids reported sounds of rustling silk and banging doors. Once again one wonders how Mr Mompesson succeeded in keeping any domestic staff at all, for they must by now have been as terrified as the children. The knocking returned again and one night one of Mr Mompesson's guests who was present suddenly stood up and spoke to the spirit. From what he said it was now clear, if it had not been so before to Mr Mompesson, that the drummer was behind it all. 'Satan,' cried the guest, 'if the drummer set thee to work give three knocks and no more!' which it did and very distinctly. Later the guest asked the spirit to confirm what he had asked him by giving five knocks 'which it did and left the house quiet all the night after'. Then the drumming began again. It was at this point that Glanvil suggested straw being strewn on the floor of the room to see if any impression was left by the spirit. In the morning they found the imprint of a great claw, together with circles, scratches, and indecipherable letters.

This was followed by the sounds of scratchings, panting, and grunting like a fierce animal. There was also a writhing about in beds, in a linen bag, under bolsters, but always unseen 'all on my own single testimony and observations', wrote Glanvil. He adds curiously, that at no single moment was he in any way afraid, only calm and determined to solve the mystery. This, he argued, could only strengthen his theories that it was an evil spirit he was dealing with. 'I know that I saw and heard all the particulars that I have here told and I am convinced that there was what we call something extraordinary and supernatural in the business.' He then tells how quite early one morning he was awakened by a loud knocking on his door, whereupon he cried out 'In the name of God who are you?' and a voice answered: 'Nothing with you.' Thinking it was one of the servants Glanvil went to sleep again, only to be told by Mr Mompesson that no servant was ever about at that time of the morning since none of them ever rose before he did. Nevertheless, Glanvil asked every one of his servants personall if they had been moving about at that time. None of them had.

The next thing to happen was a great disturbance in the fireplace of one of the rooms. Mr Mompesson fired his pistol into it and afterwards they found 'several drops of blood in the hearth and in divers places on the stairs'. Once again the spirit attacked the children, snatching away their rush lights, purring like a cat, leaping upon them as they slept, until they were so terrified, one of them taking several hours to recover, that Mr Mompesson was forced to take them away to a neighbour again. That same night Mr Mompesson heard footsteps coming up the stairs, pausing outside his room and continuing up the stair to the room where his manservant slept. The manservant woke to see a figure standing by the head of his bed: 'a great Body with two red glowing eyes, which for some time were fixed steadily upon him, and at length disappeared'. Iron bars were put into Mr Mompesson's bed, and 'a naked knife lying upright' into his mother's. There was a noise all day and most of the night with furniture hurled about, chamber pots emptied into beds, porringers broken and books hurled into ashes. Still the Mompesson household continued to live on in a house which no sane person could have tolerated, much less force wife, servants and children to suffer in as well. Mompesson emerges from this whole sequence of events as a stubborn and even stupid man. One is forced to wonder how effectively he carried out his duties as a magistrate.

In 1663 William Drury, the drummer, was arrested on a charge of stealing, tried at Salisbury Assizes and committed to Gloucester gaol. He was visited there by a man he had once known in Wiltshire. He asked his visitor what news he had from that county and the man replied that he knew of none at all. 'No?' answered the drummer, 'do you not hear of the drumming in the gentleman's house at Tedworth?' 'That I do enough' said the other. 'Aye' quoth the drummer 'I have plagued him all to that purpose and he shall never be aquiet till he has made me satisfaction for taking away my drum.' When this conversation was repeated to the prison authorities, the drummer was sent for trial again on a charge of witchcraft. The overwhelming evidence by witnesses of the events in Mr Mompesson's house were indisputable and the drummer was sentenced to that most dreaded of all sentences, transportation for life. 'But' adds Glanvil 'I know not how the drummer, either by raising storms or affrighting the seamen, he made shift to come back again but it is observable that during all the time of his restraint and absence the house was quiet, but as soon as he came back to liberty the noises returned.'

It is only at the very end of his narrative and no doubt because the information came out at the trial that we first learn anything at all about the drummer himself. He used to serve as a soldier in Cromwell's army where, amongst other things, he came across what he called 'gallant' books 'by an old fellow which was counted a wizard'. It was obviously in this way that the drummer came into contact with some form of magic or the occult and discovered himself to be psychic and familiar with poltergeists.

So many inconclusions are raised in the course of this story, that in the end we have to rely on the truth of Glanvil's statements. The strange thing is that the drummer escaped from transportation anyway, even though numbers of convicts died on the way to their destinations in the terrible ships, and very few of them survived to come back. Most difficult of all to understand is what happened when 'having his liberty the noises all began again'. Surely not even as stubborn a person as Mr Mompesson could have gone through those terrible events all over again. Perhaps he missed them so much while the demon drummer was away that he was relieved when they came back. And whatever happened to that drum? Perhaps it is all best left alone, as it seems to have been for some hundreds of years now. There have been no recent recordings of a drum being beaten at Tidworth other than those used in the annual military tattoo.

BIBLIOGRAPHY

Braddock, Joseph. *Haunted Houses* (1956)
Coxe, A. D. Hippisley. *Haunted Britain* (1973)
Day, J. W. *Here are ghosts and witches* (1954)
Griggs, F. L. *Highways and Byways in Berkshire* (1919)
Harper, C. G. *Haunted Houses* (1907)
Hole, Christina. *Haunted England* (1940)
Humphreys, A. L. *Bucklebury* (Reading, 1932)
Hutton, Edward. *Highways and Byways of Wiltshire* (1917)
Legg, Rodney. *A guide to Dorset ghosts* (Bournemouth, 1969)
Marple, Eric. *The realm of ghosts* (1964)
Morris, A. Clifford. *Rycote Reflections* (1969)
——. *The Rycote Yew* (Oxford, 1974)
Norman, Diana. *The stately ghosts of England* (1963)
O' Donnell, Elliot. *The screaming skull and other ghost stories* (1964)
Price, H. *Poltergeist over England* (1945)
Sitwell, Edith. *Bath* (1932)
Thacker, Fred S. *Kennet Country* (Oxford, 1932)
Underwood, Peter. *Gazetteer of British ghosts* (1971)
Walford, Edward. *Tales of our great families* (1877–80)